CIVIL WAR UNIFORMS
A PHOTO GUIDE

Front cover illustration: This cannon crew wear light artillery dress uniform jackets. The number three man, second from left, 'thumbs the vent', stopping it with a leather thumbstall so that the piece can be reloaded without fear of discharge by the number one man, who is holding the rammer. The number two man holds a tool used to search for pieces of burning powder bags which may be left after firing. The gun is a 6-pound Napoleon.

D1354855

1. Volunteers of the Charleston Zouave Cadets man the walls of Castle Pickney, overlooking Fort Sumter, near Charleston, in 1861, at the outbreak of war. The cadets, at present arms, wear grey uniforms with red cuffs, epaulettes, collars, caps and stripes on their trouser legs. The lieutenants wear the state regulation dark blue uniform. (National Archives).

CIVIL WAR UNIFORMS

A PHOTO GUIDE

Part One: Confederate Forces

PHILIP KATCHER

ARMS AND ARMOUR

▲2 ▼3

2. A gathering of officers from South Carolina's artillery on Sullivan's Island, in Charleston Harbor, in early 1861 finds them all in the state dark blue uniforms. Captain A. J. Green, Columbia Flying Artillery, is the man standing on the left; the officer standing to his left wears the double-breasted coat of a field grade officer, while the rest are company-grade officers. (National Archives)

3. Virginia's leading military organization of 1861 was its 1st Infantry Regiment. In the foreground of this 1859 photograph are men from the regiment's Company A (Richmond Greys), while the man in the double-breasted coat is from its Company K (Virginia Rifles). The men wear overcoats for winter over their grey jackets. (National Archives)

INTRODUCTION

Previously published as
*Soldiers Fotofax: Confederate
Forces of the American Civil War*
and *Soldiers Fotofax: Union Forces
of the American Civil War*. This
omnibus edition published in 1996

ISBN 1-85409-333-9

Arms and Armour Press
A Cassell Imprint
Wellington House, 125 Strand,
London WC2R 0BB

Distributed in the USA by
Sterling Publishing Co. Inc.,
387 Park Avenue South,
New York, NY 10016-8810.

Distributed in Australia by
Capricorn Link (Australia) Pty. Ltd,
2/13 Carrington Road, Castle Hill,
NSW 2154.

British Library Cataloguing-in-
Publication Data: a catalogue
record for this book is available
from the British Library

Line drawings by Bob Marrion
and the author.

Designed and edited by
DAG Publications Ltd. Designed
by David Gibbons; layout by Cilla
Eurich; edited by Roger Chesneau;
printed and bound in Great Britain.

One by one the Southern States, fearing that politics in the rest of the country would eventually cost them their slaves, seceded from the country founded less than a century earlier. The Southern soldiers of 1861 were enthusiastic, on the whole, in their support of the new Confederate States of America that the rebellious States formed.

In a short time, however, superior Northern and Western resources began to tell. Weapons which should have been made entirely with iron or steel components had to be made with brass; so brass became rare, and things which should have been made of brass – finials on cartridge boxes and buttons on jackets – were made of wood and lead. There was insufficient leather, so soldiers wore shoes made with cotton tops and carried percussion caps in cotton cap pouches.

These shortages began to tell not just in weapons of war, but in the 'little things'. Photographic chemicals and equipment, for example, had come from the North and grew scarcer as the war went on. Therefore, most of our photographs of Confederate soldiers were either taken early in the war, when there were still abundant supplies, or are of popular generals whose portraits could be sold to the public or else were taken by Northern photographers and show dead or captured Confederate soldiers.

Our impression of the Confederate Army and Navy is not, as a result, exact. Yet the motley array of uniforms and equipment we see in surviving photographs agrees with the written records. Fanciful volunteer uniforms from 1861 were worn until they were rags. Thereafter, soldiers often preferred uniforms and equipment from home or captured from Union Army supplies to those the government issued. Foreign visitors were sometimes amazed by the lack of uniformity in the Confederate Army, but they were just as amazed by its fighting abilities.

This is not to say that the Army and Navy had no dress regulations – only that there were as often ignored as followed. Generally, however, it is safe to say that Army officers followed regulations in wearing double-breasted grey coats with branch-of-service coloured pointed cuffs and standing colours. The average enlisted man wore a single-breasted, waist-length, plain grey jacket and most preferred light-coloured broad-brimmed hats to the regulation cap, which was a copy of the French Army cap. Sky blue uniforms were usually seen if a Union Army camp had been successfully overrun; otherwise, grey or brown prevailed.

Navy uniforms were copied from those worn in the Royal Navy, with one major difference: they were grey for both officers and sailors. This colour was not always popular with the traditionally minded seaman, and blue was worn at sea in the form of jackets and caps despite regulations.

After four years of desperate fighting, the South was finally overcome. Its legacy has lasted through to today, in films, books and 'living history' events. I wish to thank those 'living history' enthusiasts whose photographs appear in this book, as well as those who actually supplied such photographs, for their help.

Philip Katcher

◄4   5▲   6▼

. Drum Major E. R. M. Pohle of the 1st Virginia Infantry in April 1861. His grey coat is trimmed with light blue and his pompon is red, white and blue; the two-piece belt buckle bears the arms of the Commonwealth of Virginia. His sash is red, his trousers sky blue and his epaulettes fringed with brass shoulder scales. (National Archives)

5. Private J. K. Ewing, 4th Virginia Infantry, in 1861, wearing a civilian-type shirt and a 'Sicilian' cap. This cap was especially popular in Virginia in 1861 and was copied from those worn by Garibaldi's forces in Italy. Ewing's regiment became part of the famed Stonewall Brigade. Ewing himself was appointed a Second Lieutenant and was killed at Gettysburg. (Herb Peck Jr collection)

6. Volunteer units of the prewar South generally wore stock pattern badges on uniforms that varied tremendously in detail form unit to unit. The shako, as this volunteer of an unknown unit wears, was a standard uniform item, as was his dark blue or green coat, fringed epaulettes and two-piece waist belt bearing a state coat-of-arms insignia. (Author's collection)

7. Many Virginia volunteers of 1861, such as this man, wore their civilian clothing to war with only a military-type cap to show their combatant status. The cap is dark blue or green, a common colour among Virginia volunteers, with a shiny black peak and chinstrap, the latter made with a non-functional buckle. (Author's collection)

8. Rifle units were popular among volunteers. Most wore, as this man does, the vertical bugle cap badge, in this case with the regular US Army dress cap. Coats were usually dark green, although blue coats were often worn instead. The three rows of buttons were common among volunteers. (Richard Carlisle collection)

▲9 ▼10 ▼11

9. These volunteers, photographed on 10 May 1861, are members of the Clinch Rifles, which became Company A, 5th Georgia Infantry. Their shirts are civilian-pattern, but they wear their Company's dark green trousers with a gold stripe down each leg and dark green caps with a cap badge that featured a gilt wreath around the Roman letters 'CR'. (US Army Military History Institute)

10. The 5th Company of New Orleans' Washington Artillery served in the Western theatre of the war while the rest of the battalion served in the Army of Northern Virginia. These 5th Company men were photographed at Camp Lewis, near Carrolton, Louisiana, in their dark blue uniforms with red trim. The man standing has two red chevrons on each sleeve, indicating the rank of Corporal. (Library of Congress)

11. Not all prewar volunteers were elaborately uniformed. This man, who is rather elderly for active field service, wears a flannel overshirt which was common among volunteers of 1861. He holds a sword bayonet for his unusual weapon which includes the patchbox of the M1814 rifle, the barrelbands, barrel and hammer of the M1855 rifle, and the lockplate of the M1861 rifled musket. (Herb Peck Jr collection)

12. Because images in Ambrotypes and tintypes, two of the most common period photographs, were reversed (i.e., the left side appears on the right), many men reversed the position of their equipment and wore their belts upside down so that the equipment would appear on the correct side – hence this Tennessee volunteer's upside-down US belt plate. The weapon is an M1841 Mississippi rifle. (Herb Peck Jr collection)

▲13 ▼14

▲15

13. This Tennessee infantryman is armed with an M1816 smoothbore musket that has been converted from flintlock to percussion. The revolver in his belt is a Colt. The letters on his cap front apparently stand for Fayetteville Guard, which became Company G, 1st Tennessee Infantry. The regiment fought at the First Manassas, in the Peninsular Campaign and at Sharpsburg, Fredericksburg, Gettysburg, The Wilderness, Cold Harbor and Petersburg, and it surrendered at Appomattox. (Herb Peck Jr collection)

14. General Robert Edward Lee, here photographed towards the end of the war, became one of America's most famous soldiers as a result of his leadership as commander of the Army of Northern Virginia. He was a Colonel of Engineers in the US Army and when Virginia left the US he followed his state into the Confederacy. After the war he became President of Virginia's Washington College, dying there on 12 October 1870. (Library of Congress)

15. Lieutenant General A. P. Hill was a graduate of West Point (Class of 1847) who served in the Mexican-American War and entered Confederate service as Colonel of the 13th Virginia Infantry. After distinguished performances in Northern Virginia in 1862, he was named a Lieutenant General on 24 May 1863 and given command of the Third Corps of the Army of Northern Virginia. He was killed near Petersburg on 2 april 1865. (Library of Congress)

16. General Lee (seated) was photographed on the porch of his Richmond home after the Army of Northern Virginia's surrender. To the left is his son, Major General G. W. C. Lee, who commanded troops in the defence of Richmond, and to the right is the elder Lee's aide, Colonel Walter Taylor. Lee wears a grey frock coat and matching trousers, although he usually wore a short grey sack coat and blue trousers in the field. (Library of Congress)

▲17 ▼18   ▲19 ▼20

21▲

22▲

17. Lieutenant General N. B. Forrest, an uneducated man, was a brilliant cavalry commander in the Western Theatre. His troops captured Murfreesboro, Tennessee, in early 1862 and Fort Pillow in April 1864. In late 1864 his successes at Brices Cross Roads and Tupelo caused Union troops to fear for their communications. His troops were finally overwhelmed by superior forces at Selma, Alabama, in April 1865. (Library of Congress)

18. Lieutenant General J. B. Hood, one of the South's poorer commanders, lost his army in foolish attacks on Franklin and Nashville in 1864. His coat buttons are in pairs, apparently indicating the rank of Brigadier General after the US Army regulations, although CS dress regulations did not spell out differences in general officer dress. His cuffs are piped buff rather than merely buff. (Library of Congress)

19. Major General J. E. B. Stuart's frock-coat lapels are here buttoned back; his standing collar and cuffs are regulation buff. Stuart led the cavalry of the Army of Northern Virginia gallantly, although he was rather too concerned about his own reputation to be outstanding general. He died in action at Yellow Tavern, near Richmond, on 11 May 1864. (Library of Congress)

20. Major General Joseph Wheeler commanded the cavalry of the Army of Mississippi. Wounded three times in action, he rejoined the US Army during the Spanish-American War and retired as a brigadier general in 1900. His buttons are arranged in threes, which would indicate the rank of Major General in the US Army. (Library of Congress)

21. Major General George Pickett is best known for commanding the division that made the unsuccessful assault on Union Army lines at Gettysburg on 3 July 1863. His dark blue trousers are regulation, but he has disobeyed dress regulations with his dark blue collar and cuffs, the latter, uniquely, trimmed with gold embroidery. (Library of Congress)

22. Major General Mansfield Lovell was in command during the unsuccessful defence of New Orleans; thereafter he commanded a corps at Shiloh but held no other field commands. The three stars and wreath of his rank have been sewn on his all-grey coat and his buttons, in threes, apparently indicate his rank. (Library of Congress)

▲24   ▼25   26▶

▲23

23. Major General Arnold Elzy appears, in this photograph, to wear the insignia of a colonel; indeed, he served as Colonel of the 1st Maryland Regiment until promoted to brigadier general after the First Manassas. However, the faint four lines of a general officer's Austrian knot appear on each sleeve. The narrow gold lace on his shoulder is designed to hold a fringed gold epaulette in place. (Library of Congress)

24. Major General Benjamin Huger, an ordnance officer in the US Army before the Civil War, was relieved of field command after an inept performance on 12 July 1862. Thereafter he served successfully as an inspector of artillery and ordnance, mainly in the Trans-Mississippi Department. (US Army Military History Institute)

25. Brigadier General B. F. Cheatham served as a brigade, division, and corps commander in every battle the Army of Tennessee fought. His buttons are arranged in pairs; the standing collar of his waistcoat, which is probably buff in accordance with regulations, is folded down. His collar insignia is strictly regulation. (Library of Congress)

26. Major General William Mahone, a corps commander in the Army of Northern Virginia, wears a type of short jacket which was popular with Confederate generals in the field as a comfortable riding habit. His grey or tan slouch hat, with its non-regulation badge, was also the most common field wear for all ranks. (National Archives)

◀27　▲28　▼29

27. P. G. T. Beaureguard, here in the all-dark-blue uniform of a colonel of engineers in the Louisiana Army, had been breveted twice for bravery as an engineer staff officer during the Mexican-American War. He was in command at the Siege of Fort Sumter and was second in command at the First Manassas and Shiloh. A personality conflict with Jefferson Davis resulted in his never getting the top command he possibly could have handled. (Author's collection)

28. James Kemper was photographed here as Colonel of the 7th Virginia Infantry, which he commanded from the First Manassas to the Peninsular Campaign. He was promoted to Brigadier General on 3 June 1862 and was wounded and captured in Pickett's Charge at Gettysburg. The laydown collar (as opposed to the regulation standing collar) was common among Confederate officers, as was the absence of any coat trim other than collar rank badges. (Library of Congress)

29. Colonel John Gregg commanded the 7th Texas Infantry Regiment from its formation until he was wounded at Chickamauga. After recovering he was promoted to command the Texas Brigade of the Army of Northern Virginia and was killed 7 October 1864. Greg's plain grey frock coat lacks collar insignia, a practice allowed in the field after 3 June 1862. (Herb Peck Jr collection)

30. The three white officers are surgeons, while the black man appears to be their servant. One wears the common field sack coat. Confederate surgeons often had to make do with replacement supplies, as medicines had come from outside the South before the war and the blockade hindered resupply, surgeons having to use home-made cotton or flax thread instead. (US Army Military History Institute)

31. Major J. S. Mosby was one of the South's most noted partisan leaders. His troops, designated the 43rd Independent Virginia Cavalry Battalion, operated behind Union lines in northern Virginia, forcing the use of large numbers of Union troops to protect the area. Here he wears a sack coat with an Austrian knot on each sleeve and holds a light slouch hat. (Library of Congress)

32. Captain James Tucker, 9th Florida Infantry Regiment, holding a dark-coloured slouch hat. The 9th was formed in Virginia in June 1864, largely from the old 6th Florida Infantry Battalion. It served in the Army of Northern Virginia until its surrender on 9 April 1865; Tucker was one of fifteen officers in the unit at the time. (Fritz Kirsch)

33. First Lieutenant Charles Harper was said to have been the first man killed from Guilford County, North Carolina. His volunteer's uniform is dark blue, with US Army-style shoulder straps worn to indicate rank. His forage cap is decorated with gold lace according to Confederate dress regulations for his rank. (US Army Military History Institute)

34. It was definitely against regulations to wear US Army-style shoulder straps to indicate rank, according to the 21 March 1861 Richmond *Daily Dispatch*. Yet Second Lieutenant J. B. Washington (seen here on the left), an aide to confederate General J. E. Johnston, was captured on 31 May 1862 and photographed then in a grey jacket with yellow trim around the collar, down the front and around each pocket and US Army shoulder strap rank insignia. (Library of Congress)

▲35 ▼36

▲37 ▼38

39▲

40▲

35. This unidentifie first lieutenant of infantry was photographed in New Orleans in a perfectly regulation uniform, complete with double-breasted frock coat with sky blue facings and a matching kepi with gold lace to indicate rank. The Austrian knot on each sleeve is faint but visible on the original print. (John Wernick)

36. First Lieutenant W. H. Young, an infantry officer from North Carolina, wears an unusually plain single-breasted jacket with gilt buttons and two gold bars on his collar to indicate rank. Each sleeve is marked with a gold Austrian knot, and his matching trousers have a dark stripe down each

leg. His apparently dark blue cap is piped with light blue. (US Army Military History Institute)

37. This officer, apparently from Louisiana, wears a US Army belt plate with its silver wreath around a gilt eagle. His pistol holster is made with the pistol butt facing the rear; most had the butt facing the front. Most Confederate officers attempted to follow dress regulations. (John Wernick)

38. Enlisted men were rarely able to follow dress regulations by wearing double-breasted frock coats. Nevertheless, this non-commissioned officer has managed to obtain one, albeit without coloured collar or cuffs.

The star over the chevrons should indicate the rank of Ordnance Sergeant, but similar stars were worn unofficially by large numbers of colour sergeants. (US Army Military History Institute)

39. While regulations offered no special insignia for company quartermaster sergeants, some followed the lead of the US Army in using the chevrons worn here by Company Quartermaster Sergeant Archibald Johnston, The British Guard. The Mobile, Alabama, unit was a local defence force that was captured on the city's fall in 1865. (Ernest Brown collection)

40. Sergeant Page Baker, Louisiana Guards, 1st Special Battalion, Louisiana Infantry, wears what appears to be a lieutenant's cap with his sergeant's jacket. The epaulettes, collar, cuffs and chevrons may be black or red; black was a common colour for sergeant's chevrons regardless of branch of service. Such trimmed jackets were rare after 1862. (US Army Military History Institute)

A: The British-made P1853 Enfield rifled musket, and its later variations, was the standard infantry longarm in the Confederate Army.

B: This copy of the British Army's knapsack was made by S. Isaacs, Campbell, in London for the Confederate Army. The company had been formed for the sole purpose of producing military supplies for the South. The knapsack was made of black rubberized canvas with leather corner reinforcing.

C: The Louisiana belt plate, as worn by the Louisiana Tigers and other Louisiana troops, featured a pelican feeding its young in a nest. The belt plate was a solid brass casting.

D: All the rifled muskets and carbines made by the London Armoury were produced for the Confederate Army. This is the lockplate of one of the company's rifled muskets.

E: This Confederate-made tin canteen is a copy of the US Army-issue canteen. It uses a carved wooden stopper instead of the US Army's cork stopper and its strap is a converted musket sling.

F: This novel drum-style, Southern-made canteen was produced by nailing together two shaped pieces of wood. The original is in the Confederate Museum in Richmond, Virginia.

G: Most Southern-made wooden canteens resembled small barrels. This one has a leather strap, but coarse cotton straps which could not be adjusted for different lengths were also used.

H: Wheat's Louisiana Tigers were recruited from among the Irish along the docks of New Orleans in 1861 and fought well at the First Manassas. After their commander was so badly wounded that he could no longer serve during the Peninsula campaign, the unit fell apart for lack of discipline. The jackets were dark blue with red trim; the fezzes were red with blue tassels; the trousers were blue and white striped (some say that they were made of bed ticking); and the gaiters were white.

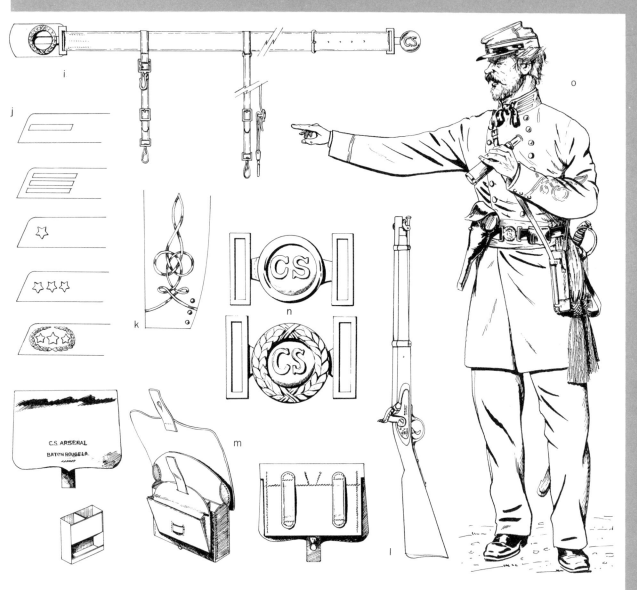

I: A typical example of an officer's sword belt. Examples in both russet brown and black leather are known, although black was the regulation colour. The two-piece belt plate was worn by mounted men as well as officers.

J: Officers' collar insignia were worn on branch-of-service coloured collars. The ranks indicated are (from the top) Second Lieutenant, Captain, Major, Colonel and General. The same insignia were worn by brigadier generals, major generals, lieutenant generals and generals.

K: The gold Austrian knot was worn on each officer's sleeve. The single braid here indicates a lieutenant; two knots, a captain; three, a field-grade officer; and four, a general-grade officer.

L: The British-made P1858 cavalry carbine was the most common Confederate carbine. This particular example was made by the London firm of Barnett.

M: This cartridge box for the 0.58-calibre rifled musket was made by the Confederate arsenal in Baton Rouge, Louisiana. It came with a single pair of loops, so that it could be carried on the waist belt, and an inner pouch for musket tools and patches. Two tin containers, as shown on the left, kept the ammunition safe.

N: The most common mounted man's and officer's belt plate bore the letters 'CS' within a wreath; the variation on top was less common but still worn, while a still rarer variation used the letters 'CSA' within the wreath.

O: The rank of this captain in regulation dress is indicated by the two stripes on the front, sides and back of his kepi; the three bars on his collar; and the two stripes in his Austrian knot on his sleeves. His sword is a foot officer's style, indicating that he is in the foot artillery or infantry.

CHRONOLOGY

Note: Some battles received different names from the opposing sides; for example, what the Confederates called Sharpsburg the Union forces called Antietam. Confederate names have been used in this list.

1860
6 November: Abraham Lincoln elected US President.
20 December: South Carolina votes to leave the US.
31 December: The US government refuses to abandon its property in South Carolina, despite state demands that it do so.

1861
9 January: Mississippi votes to leave the US.
10 January: Florida votes to leave the US.
11 January: Alabama votes to leave the US.
19 January: Georgia votes to leave the US.
26 January: Louisiana votes to leave the US.
1 February: Texas votes to leave the US.
7 February: The Choctaw Indian Nation votes to side with the South.
9 February: Jefferson Davis and Alexander Stephens elected President and Vice-President respectively of the Provincial Government of the Confederate States of America.
19 February: Confederate government formed in Montgomery, Alabama.
21 February: CS Navy authorized.
4 March: First national 'stars and bars' flag adopted.
6 March: CS Army authorized.
11 March: CS Constitution adopted.
16 March: CS Marine Corps authorized.
19 April: War Department orders Army uniform of dark blue smocks, steel grey trousers, forage caps and red or white shirts.
12–13 April: Siege of Fort Sumter, South Carolina (CS victory).
17 April: Virginia votes to leave the US.
6 May: Arkansas and Tennessee join the Confederacy.
20 May: North Carolina votes to leave the US.
21 May: Richmond, Virginia, is named capital of the CSA.
6 June: Final Army dress regulations published.
21 July: Battle of First Manassas (CS victory).
10 August: Battle of Wilson's Creek, Missouri (CS victory).
19 August: Missouri forms alliance with CSA.
22 October: Beginning of New Mexico invasion.
29 November: Missouri admitted into CSA.
9 December: Kentucky admitted into CSA.

1862
18 January: Confederate Territory of Arizona formed.
6–16 February: Forts Henry and Donelson fall (US victory).
21 February: Capture of Albuquerque and Sante Fe, New Mexico (CS victory).
22 February: CS government named Permanent and no longer Provisional.
6–8 March: Battle of Pea Ridge, Arkansas (US victory).
9 March: USS *Monitor* stands off CSS *Virginia* (US victory).
23 March: Battle of Kernstown, Virginia (US victory).
5 April–2 July: Peninsula campaign against Richmond (CS victory).
6–7 April: Battle of Shiloh, Tennessee (US victory).

7 April: Island Number 10 falls (US victory).
11 April: Fort Pulaski, Georgia, falls (US victory).
19 April: Army Signal Corps authorized.
29 April: New Orleans, Louisiana, falls (US victory).
1 June: Robert E. Lee given command of Army of Northern Virginia.
3 June: Army caps to be made with dark blue bands and rest in branch-of-service colours, with rank markings for officers; officers allowed to dispense with collar insignia in the field.
23 July: Regiments allowed to inscribe battle honours on colours.
29 July: Cruiser CSS *Alabama* launched at Birkenhead, England.
26–30 August: Battle of Second Manassas (CS victory).
14 September: Battle of South Mountain (standoff).
17 September: Battle of Sharpsburg (draw, but an effective US victory).
24 September: Great Seal of the Confederacy adopted.
8 October: Battle of Perryville (US victory).
20 November: Army of Tennessee organized.
13 December: Battle of Fredericksburg, Virginia (CS victory).
24 December: Fall of Galveston, Texas.
31 December–2 January: Battle of Murfreesboro (US victory).

1863
3 March: Day of national fasting and prayer.
23 March: CS Naval Academy founded.
1 May: Second national flag adopted.
1–3 May: Battle of Chancellorsville, Virginia (CS victory).
10 May: Major General T. J. ('Stonewall') Jackson dies.
16 May: Battle of Champion's Hill, Mississippi (US victory).
19 May–4 July: Siege of Vicksburg, Mississippi (US victory).
27 May–9 July: Siege of Port Hudson, Louisiana (US victory).
9 June: Battle of Brandy Station, Virginia (draw).
19 June: Volunteer CSN officers to wear gilt letters 'VN' on cap fronts.
1–3 July: Battle of Gettysburg (US victory).
17 July: Battle of Honey Springs, Indian Territory (US victory).
11 August: Large pro-US meeting held in Washington, North Carolina.
19–20 September: Battle of Chickamauga (CS victory).
25 November: Battle of Missionary Ridge, Tennessee (US victory).
26–28 November: Mine Run Campaign (CS victory).

1864
17 February: Army Invalid Corps authorized.
20 February: Battle of Olustee, Florida (CS victory).
27 February: Prisoner-of-war camp opened at Andersonville, Georgia.
5 May: Wilderness campaign begins; fighting in Virginia will not end until Lee surrenders.
11 May: J. E. B. Stuart mortally wounded.
13 May: Battle of Resaca; first major battle in Atlanta campaign.
10 June: Battle of Brice's Crossroads, Mississippi (CS victory); Congress authorizes drafting of men aged 17 to 50.
19 June: CSS *Alabama* sunk off French coast.
2–14 July: Early's Raid against Washington, DC (US victory).
20 July: Battle of Winchester, Virginia (US victory).
22 July: Battle of Atlanta, Georgia (US victory).
5 August: Battle of Mobile Bay, Alabama (US victory).
1 September: Atlanta abandoned.
8 October: Cruiser CSS *Shenandoah* sails from England.

15 November–10 December: Sherman's troops march from Atlanta to Savannah on the Atlantic coast.

25 November: Plot to burn New York City fails.

20 December: Savannah abàndoned.

1865

15 January: Fort Fisher, North Carolina (last Southern port open) falls.

6 February: Robert E. Lee named General-in-Chief of the Armies of the Confederate States.

18 February: Charleston, South Carolina, falls.

2 March: Lee writes to Grant proposing meeting to discuss peace negotiations; offer is refused.

4 March: Last national flag adopted.

6 March: Battle of Natural Bridge, Florida (CS victory).

13 March: Blacks authorized to serve in the Army.

18 March: CS Congress adjourns for last time.

19–21 March: Battle of Bentonville, North Carolina (last major battle of the war: US victory).

1 April: Battle of Five Forks, Virginia (US victory).

3 April: Richmond, Virginia, falls.

9 April: Army of Northern Virginia surrenders to Army of the Potomac.

12 April: Mobile, Alabama (last major Southern city in Confederate hands) falls.

26 April: General Joseph Johnston's army surrenders in North Carolina.

26 May: Trans-Mississippi command surrenders.

6 November: CSS *Shenandoah* surrenders to British authorities.

ARMIES AND CORPS OF THE CONFEDERACY

Army of the Shenandoah: Formed near Harper's Ferry, Virginia, 21 April 1861. Merged into the Army of the Potomac July 1861. Commanders: Maj. Gen. K. Harper; Col. T. J. Jackson; Brig. Gen. J. E. Johnston.

Army of the Peninsula: Formed 26 May 1861. Merged into the Army of Potomac 12 April 1862. Commander: Col. J. B. Magruder.

Army of the Northwest: Formed in Western Virginia 8 June 1861 and dissolved 9 February 1862. Commanders: Brig. Gens. R. S. Garnett and H. R. Jackson; Maj. Gens. W. W. Loring, E. Johnson.

Army of the Potomac: Formed 24 May 1861 in Northern Virginia; merged into Army of Northern Virginia 1 June 1862. Commanders: Gens. P. G. T. Beaureguard, J. E. Johnston.

Army of Northern Virginia: Formed 1 June 1862; surrendered 9 April 1865. Commander: Gen. Robert E. Lee.

I Corps: Formed 6 November 1862. Commanders: Lt. Gen. J. Longstreet; Maj. Gen. R. H. Anderson.

II Corps: Formed 6 November 1862. Commanders: Lt. Gens. T. J. Jackson, R. S. Ewell, J. A. Early, J. B. Gordon.

III Corps: Formed 30 May 1863. Commander: Lt. Gen. A. P. Hill.

IV Corps: Formed 19 October 1864. Commander: Lt. Gen. R. H. Anderson.

Cavalry Corps: Formed 30 May 1863. Commanders: Maj. Gens. J. E. B. Stuart, Fitzhugh Lee; Lt. Gen. Wade Hampton.

Army of the Kanawha: Formed 11 August 1861 in Western Virginia; dissolved early 1862. Commander: Brig. Gen. J. B. Floyd.

Army of Eastern Kentucky: Formed from local militia 1861; dissolved 1862. Commander: Brig. Gen. H. Marshall.

Army of New Mexico: Formed in Texas 14 December 1861; dissolved in December 1862. Commander: Brig. Gen. H. H. Sibley.

Army of Louisiana: Formed from Louisiana State troops 1861 and dissolved shortly afterwards. Commander: Brig. Gen. P. O. Hebert.

Army of Pensacola: Formed near Pensacola, Florida, 22 October 1861; dissolved after that town's evacuation 9 May 1862. Commander: Brig. Gen. A. H. Gladden.

Army of Mobile: Formed near Mobile, Alabama, 27 January 1862; dissolved 27 June 1862. Commander: Maj. Gen. J. M. Withers.

Central Army of Kentucky: Formed in Kentucky September 1861; merged into Army of the Mississippi 29 March 1862. Commanders: Lt. Gens. S. B. Buckner, A. S. Johnston.

Army of East Tennessee/Kentucky: Formed February 1862 near Knoxville; redesignated Army of Kentucky 25 August 1862; merged into Army of Tennessee as Smith's Corps 20 November 1862. Commander: Gen. E. K. Smith.

Army of the Mississippi/Tennessee: Formed in Western Department 5 March 1862; became Army of Tennessee 7 November 1862; surrendered 26 April 1865. Commanders: Gens. A. S. Johnston, P. G. T. Beauregard, B. Bragg, J. E. Johnston, J. B. Hood; Maj. Gens. W. J. Hardee, L. Polk.

I Corps: Formed 5 March 1862. Commanders: Maj. Gens. L. Polk, W. J. Hardee, B. F. Cheatham.

II Corps: Formed 5 March 1862. Commanders: Maj. Gens. B. Bragg, S. Jones, W. J. Hardee, J. C. Breckinridge, D. H. Hill, S. D. Lee.

III Corps: Never an official unit, it existed as a tactical formation. Commanders: Maj. Gens. W. J. Hardee, L. Polk, A. P. Stewart, E. D. Walthall.

Cavalry Corps: Formed 22 January 1863. Commander: Maj. Gen. W. J. Wheeler.

Army of Middle Tennessee: Formed 28 October 1862; merged into Army of Tennessee. Commander: Maj. Gen. J. C. Breckinridge.

Army of the West: Formed 29 Janaury 1862; later merged into Army of West Tennessee. Commanders: Maj. Gens. E. Van Dorn, J. P. McCowan.

Army of West Tennessee/Mississippi: Formed 20 June 1862; surrendered 4 July 1863. Commander: Lt. Gen. J. C. Pemberton.

Southern Army/Trans-Mississippi Army: Formed in West Lousiana and Texas 14 January 1863; surrendered 26 May 1865. Commanders: Lt. Gens. T. H. Holmes, R. Taylor.

Army of Missouri: Formed August 1864; later merged into Trans-Mississippi Army. Commander: Maj. Gen. S. Price.

Army of Mississippi: Formed December 1863 in Alabama, Mississippi, and East Louisiana; merged into Army of Tennessee 26 July 1864. Commanders: Lt. Gen. A. P. Stewart; Maj. Gen. E. C. Walthall.

UNIFORMS OF THE CONFEDERATE FORCES

Army and Marine Corps Commissioned Officers' Insignia

Gold embroidery worn on the front part of the coat collar:

General Officers: A wreath enclosing three stars, the centre one 1¼in and the others ¾in in diameter.

Colonel: Three stars arranged horizontally.

Lieutenant Colonel: Two stars arranged horizontally.
Major (Surgeon): One star.
Captain (Assistant Surgeon): Three horizontal ½in bars.
First Lieutenant: Two horizontal ½in bars.
Second Lieutenant: One horizontal ½in bar.

Gold braid worn on each coat sleeve in the form of an Austrian knot and on the top, sides, back and front of the cap:
General Officers: Four braids.
Field Grade Officers: Three braids.
Captains (Assistant Surgeons): Two braids.
Lieutenants: One braid.

Branch of Service Colours
Worn by all ranks on coat collars and cuffs and caps and as stripes on trousers by regimental officers and sergeants:
Infantry: Sky blue.
Artillery: Red.
Cavalry: Yellow.
General Officers, Staff, Engineers: Buff (dark blue caps).
Medical Department: Black.
Marines: Dark blue.

Sashes
Worn by officers and sergeants:
General Officers: Buff.
Staff, Engineers, Artillery, Infantry, Marine Corps: Red.
Cavalry: Yellow.
Medical Department: Green.

Army and Marine Corps Enlisted Sleeve Insignia
Chevrons worn above the elbow in branch-of-service colours for Army, points down, and in black, points up, for Marines:
Sergeant Major: Three bars and an arc.
Quartermaster Sergeant: Three bars and a tie.
Ordnance Sergeant: Three bars and a star.
First (Orderly) Sergeant: Three bars and a lozenge.
Sergeant: Three bars in worsted.
Hospital Steward (Army only; unofficial): Three bars and a lozenge in black.

Army Cap Badges
No cap badges were known to have been adopted officially, yet some were known to have been worn:
Surgeon: Old English letters 'MS', often within a wreath.
Ambulance Corpsman: Red cloth badge.
Signal Corps: White metal crossed signal flags.

Army Trouser Stripes
Worn on the outside leg of sky blue trousers for regimental officers and other ranks and dark blue trousers for other officers:
General officers: Two ⅝in gold stripes, ⅛in apart.
Staff, Engineers: One 1¼in gold stripe.
Surgeons: A 1¼in black velvet stripe edged with gold.
Regimental Officers: A 1¼in branch-of-service coloured stripe.
Sergeants: As for regimental officers.

CONFEDERATE NAVY DRESS REGULATIONS

Navy Relative Rank
There were two types of Navy officers, executive (deck) and civil. Each type had a unique title, but they all wore basically the same uniform, with differences indicated by the colour of the gold-edged shoulder straps and the 'executive loop' worn on the upper bar of executive officer cuff lace:
Admiral: Only an executive officer rank.
Flag officer: Only an executive officer rank.
Captain: Only an executive officer rank.
Commander: Surgeon, Paymaster, Chief Engineer or Naval Constructor over 12 years.
Lieutenant Commanding: Only an executive officer rank.
First Lieutenant: Surgeon, Paymaster, Chief Engineer or Naval Constructor under 12 years.
Second Lieutenant: Only an executive officer rank.
Master: Passed Assistant Surgeon, First Assistant Engineer.
Passed Midshipman: Assistant Surgeon or Paymaster, Second or Third Assistant Engineer.
Midshipman: Only an executive officer rank.

Naval Officer Branch of Service Colours
Each Navy officer wore a rectangular shoulder strap 4½in long and 1⅜in wide on each shoulder, edged with gold embroidery and bearing his rank insignia in gold within, on a ground of a different colour according to branch of service:
Executive Officers: Sky blue.
Medical Officers: Black.
Paymasters: Dark Green.
Engineers: Dark blue.
Naval Constructors: Buff.

Naval Officer Shoulder Strap Insignia
Admiral:* Five stars.
Flag Officer: Four stars.
Captain: Three stars.
Commander: Two stars.
Lieutenant commanding:* Two stars.
First Lieutenant:* One star.
Second Lieutenant:* Plain.
Master: Plain.
Passed Midshipman: A gold strip 4in long and ½in wide.
Civil officers over 12 years: Two crossed olive or live oak sprigs.**
Civil officers under 12 years: One olive or live oak sprig.**
Civil officers ranked with masters: Two olive leaves.***
Civil officers ranked with Passed Midshipmen: Plain***
*After 1862. **Olive worn by surgeons and paymasters, live oak by engineers and naval constructors. ***No insignia given for engineers.

Naval Officers' Cuff Lace Insignia
Bars of ½in-wide gold lace worn around each cuff to indicate rank. The top bar was looped, after the style worn by officers of the Royal Navy but ending in more of a point, with lace worn by executive officers.

	1861	1862	Naval Officer Cap Badges
Admiral*	—	Five	Admiral: Gold wreath, fouled anchor, five stars.
Flag Officer	Four	Four	Flag Officer: As above with four stars.
Captain	Three	Three	Captain: As above with three stars.
Commander	Two	Two	Commander: As above with two stars.
Lieutenants			Lieutenant Commanding: As above with two stars.
Commanding*	Two	Two	First Lieutenant: As above with one star.
Lieutenant	One	One**	Second Lieutenant: As above with no stars.
Second Lieutenant*	—	One	Master: As above with no stars.
Master	One***	One	Passed Midshipman: Plain fouled anchor.
Passed Midshipman	3 large buttons	3 large buttons	Civil officer over 12 years: Gold wreath and three stars.*
Midshipman	3 medium buttons	3 medium buttons	Civil officer under 12 years: As above with two stars.*

*Rank created in 1862. **Redesignated First Lieutenant in 1862. ***Lace was ¼in wide.

Civil officer rating as Lieutenant: As above with one star.
Civil officer rating below Lieutenant: As above with no stars.
*Engineers also wore the letter 'E' and Naval Construtors the letter 'C' under the stars within the wreath.

THE CONFEDERATE ARMED FORCES IN STATISTICS

Combat Units of the Confederate Army

Cavalry Regiments	137
Cavalry Battalions*	143
Cavalry Legions**	1
Independent Cavalry Companies	101
Artillery Regiments	16
Artillery Battalions	25
Independent Artillery Companies	227
Infantry Regiments	642
Infantry Battalions	163
Infantry Legions	9
Independent Infantry Companies	62

*A battalion had two fewer companies than a regiment – a practice dating from the eighteenth century when the two regimental flank companies, one of grenadiers and the other of light infantry, were removed, to leave the battalion as a main combat unit. **A legion was a combined-arms force including cavalry, artillery and infantry in different proportions.

Strength of the Confederate Army
Estimated total enlistments
1,227,890 to 1,406,678

Losses in the Confederate Army
Note: Because of the destruction of many official documents on the war's end, figures are not exact, but estimated.

Killed	52,954*
Died of wounds	21,570
Died of disease	59,297

*Excludes Alabama figures; better total estimate is some 94,000.

Top Ten Fighting Regiments
(as indicated by battle losses)

Regiment	Battle	Losses (%)
1st Texas	Sharpsburg	82.3
21st Georgia	Manassas	76.0
26th North Carolina	Gettysburg	71.7
6th Mississippi	Shiloh	70.5
8th Tennessee	Stone's River	68.2
10th Tennessee	Chickamauga	68.0
Palmetto Sharpshooters	Glendale	67.7
17th South Carolina	Manassas	66.9
23rd South Carolina	Manassas	66.2
44th Georgia	Mechanicsville	65.1

THE CONFEDERATE NAVY (AUGUST 1862)

Wooden converted war vessels	44
Navy-built wooden war vessels	12
Partially-built vessels	9
Navy-built iron-clad war vessels	12
Vessels being built currently	23

Strengths of the Confederate Navy

	Officers	Ratings
1861	79	Unknown
1864	753	3,674

Strengths of the Confederate Marine Corps

Year	Total (officers and men)
1861	350
1862	560
1864	539

WEAPONS OF THE CONFEDERATE ARMY

Note: Quoted material and numbers are taken from the Ordnance Field Manual, published by the Confederate Army in Richmond in 1862.

FIELD ARTILLERY
Gun Howitzer, Bronze (Napoleon): Smoothbore. Tube bronze; weight 788lb; length 58.6in; range (at 3° 45′ elevation) 1,300yd. Firing a 12lb shot, this was the preferred Confederate field artillery piece.

Gun Howitzer, Iron (1862 field model): Smoothbore. Tube iron; weight 850lb; length 64.4in; range (at 3° 30′ elevation) 1,200yd. An adaptation of the Napoleon which used iron instead of the scarcer bronze.

10-pound Parrott: Rifled. Tube iron; length 72.8in; range (at 6°) 1,950yd. Similar to the 3in rifle save for a band around the breech, this US Army weapon was highly accurate at long range. Some 3in rifles were converted into Parrott guns by having an iron band applied at the breech at Richmond's Tredegar works.

3-inch rifle (M1861): Rifled. Tube iron; weight 967lb; length 67in; range (at 6°) 2,250yd. Firing a 10lb shot, this weapon was especially accurate at long range and good for counter-battery work.

INFANTRY LONGARMS
M1841 Rifle (Mississippi): Rifled; 0.54-calibre. Length 52.66in; barrel length

33in. Browned barrel and lock; brass mountings. A common early war weapon, taking a sabre bayonet.

M1842 Musket: Smoothbore; 0.69-calibre. Length 57.75in; barrel length 42in. Bright-finished iron furniture. Although obsolete, this weapon was often issued, especially in the early years of the war.

M1855 Rifled Musket: Rifled; 0.58-calibre. Length 74in; barrel length 40in. Bright-finished iron furniture. The Richmond Armory produced 11,762 copies of this US Army weapon.

M1855 Rifle: Rifled; 0.55-calibre. Length 72in; barrel length 33in. Iron barrel and lock; brass mountings. The Fayetteville Armory, North Carolina, made some 20,000 copies of this US Army weapon.

P1853 Rifled Musket (Enfield): Rifled; 0.577-calibre. Length 55in; barrel length 39in. Bright-finished iron barrel and lock; brass mountings. The regulation British Army longarm of the period. The Confederates imported some 115,000 of these weapons from Britain as well as making perhaps 20,000 copies in the South.

M1854 Lorenz Rifled Musket: Rifled; 0.54-calibre. Length 52.7in. Bright iron finish. The regulation Austrian Army weapon of the period. The Confederates imported about 100,000 of this somewhat crude weapon.

CARBINES

M1855: Rifled; muzzle-loading; 0.58-calibre. Length 41.5in. Bright iron finish. A cut-down version of the Richmond Armory's M1855 rifled musket. Some 19,764 were made until the machinery for manufacturing the weapons was shipped to Tallahassee, Alabama, in mid-1864.

P1856 Carbine (Enfield): Muzzle-loading; 0.577-calibre. Length 37in. Iron lock and barrel; brass mountings. This British Army weapon was both widely imported and manufactured in the South. It was eventually named as the regulation cavalry carbine, and the Government's Tallahassee Armory in Alabama produced some 900 examples by the end of the war.

M1859 Sharps: Rifled; breech-loading; 0.52-calibre. Length 37.75in. Polished iron metal parts. The basic method of obtaining these highly sought-after weapons was by capture from the US Army. However, a private factory, later taken over by the Government, was set

up in Richmond and eventually made some 5,200 copies of this weapon.

REVOLVERS

M1860 Colt Army: 0.44-calibre. Length 14in. A US Army weapon, but prewar supplies and wartime captures allowed this to be a standard cavalry hand gun.

M1851 Colt Navy: 0.36-calibre. Length 13in. Some 15,800 Southern-made copies of this US Army hand gun were produced. With large numbers in the South before the war and the capture of quantities of the weapon during the war, this became the standard Confederate cavalryman's and officer's hand gun. Southern-made versions often replaced the iron frames with brass and eliminated the cap guards behind the cylinders.

Grape-shot Pistol: 0.40-calibre (9 rounds); 16-gauge (one round). Barrel length 7in. An odd weapon with a cylinder revolving around another barrel which fired a load of buckshot, the LeMat was invented by a dentist from New Orleans and was produced for the Confederate Army and Navy in Britain and France. Some 2,500 were made.

EDGED WEAPONS

Cavalry Sabre: Length 43.25in; brass hilt with leather-wrapped wooden grips; blade width 1.1in in the middle; metal scabbard. Officially, 'Curved blade 36 inches long, hilt guard and scabbard of sheet steel'. These weapons were

usually crude copies of the US M1840 or M1861 cavalry sabres, with reddish brass hilts.

Mounted Artillery Sabre: Length 38.6in; single brass guard and leather-wrapped grips; blade width 1.06in in the middle; metal scabbard. Officially, 'This differs from the cavalry sabre in having a blade only 32 inches long, though of greater curvature. It also has a hilt, guard and scabbard'. Again copies of the US M1840 light artillery sabre, few of these weapons were made or issued.

Foot Artillery Sword: Length 26in; all-brass hilt; blade width 1.8in in the middle; leather scabbard. Officially, 'Has a straight two-edged blade 19 inches long, narrower near the hilt than in the middle, a hilt and leather scabbard'. A copy of the US Army M1833 foot artillery sword and a weapon virtually never seen in use.

Infantry Sword: Length 38.75in; all-brass hilt; blade width 0.72in in the middle; leather scabbard. Officially, 'Has a blade straight (cut and thrust) 32 inches in length, a hilt, guard and leather scabbard. This sword is for the non-commissioned officers of foot troops. The sword for officers not mounted is of the same pattern, with ornamented mountings'. The NCO sword was rarely seen, and most officers used copies of the US Army M1850 line officer's sword with its slightly curved blade rather than the straight blade of the NCO's sword.

41. Early-war uniforms were often elaborately trimmed, usually in black or red. This corporal's jacket has false epaulettes made simply by sewing lace in epaulette form on each shoulder. His unit is unknown. The same trim is used around the cuffs and collar and jacket edges as well as on each trouser leg. (Author's collection)

43▲ 44▼

42▲

42. The collar and cuffs on this soldier's frock coat appear to be light blue, making the coat a regulation infantry enlisted man's model. These were very rare, the few regulation enlisted frock coats seen usually being worn by heavy artillerymen in fixed posts along the Atlantic coast. (US Army Military History Institute)

43. The typical enlisted soldier's clothing for most of the war included plain grey or brown trousers and matching single-breasted jacket with between five and nine buttons down the front. Plain matching epaulettes were common as well. Buttons were often of wood rather than regulation brass. (Author's collection)

44. The plain iron or brass frame buckle, as worn on this infantryman's waist belt, was the most common Confederate Army-issue belt plate. His other equipment includes a percussion cap pouch and plain leather bayonet scabbard. His weapon is an M1842 0.69-calibre smoothbore musket. His frock coat has been trimmed around the collar and down the front, probably in black or red. (Herb Peck Jr collection)

◀ 45

46

48 ▲

49 ▲

45. Private John T. Davis of Alabama wears an all grey or light brown version of the US Army's sack coat and matching trousers. His weapon is a British-made copy of the Enfield rifled musket; his bayonet scabbard, percussion cap pouch and cartridge box are on his waist belt, as was typical of Confederate infantrymen. (US Army Military History Institute)

46. The single-shot smoothbore pistol here is probably a photographer's prop. The soldiers' grey frock coats appear to have black or red collars, the soldier with the pistol having plain cuffs and the other one with cuffs that match his collar. Their unit is unknown, but their dress is typical of that worn in 1861–62 by Southern troops. (Herb Peck Jr collection)

47. Private John Reily, 16th Mississippi Infantry Regiment,

wears a plain grey double-breasted frock coat. The 16th was organized in Corinth, Mississippi, in June 1861, and served in the Army of Northern Virginia from the Seven Days' Battle until it was surrendered at Appomattox. At Chancellorsville, 76 per cent of its men were casualties. (John R. Love collection/US Army Military History Institute)

48. The bowie knife with the D-guard was typical of personal weapons carried by Southern troops for several months after joining the army; it was, however, quickly abandoned. The shotgun, too, was probably replaced by a single-shot rifled musket. The drum canteen made of tin, however, was the most common piece of Southern military equipment carried throughout the war. (Herb Peck Jr collection)

49. Private S. C. Williams served both in Company D, 5th North Carolina State Troops and Company D, 13th North Carolina Light Artillery; it is not known which unit he was in when this photograph was taken. The 5th was organized in July 1861, fighting at the First Manassas and then through

Appomattox. The 13th was organized in December 1863, Company D serving with the Army of Tennessee and at the unsuccessful Battle of Bentonville, after which the remainder of that force surrendered. (US Army Military History Institute)

50. The star on this young soldier's belt plate may stand for Texas, but it might just as well stand for Mississippi, whose troops wore buttons bearing a five-pointed star. The soldier's equipment has been reversed,

his cartridge box normally being worn on the rear right hip and the bayonet scabbard on the left. His weapon is an M1855 rifled musket. (Herb Peck Jr collection)

51. Private William Ridley enlisted in Petersburg, Virginia, and was killed at Malvern Hill during the Peninsular Campaign. His grey forage cap bears his company letter, F, and his plain grey jacket is made with epaulettes, a common practice. Soldiers in the field almost never wore ties, as he does, and, indeed, white shirts like this were also rare. (US Army Military History Institute)

52. Northern photographers took most of the known pictures of Confederate soldiers – and the soldiers were all too often dead when their photographs were taken. These men were members of Starke's Louisiana Brigade, made up of the 1st, 2nd, 9th, 10th, and 15th Louisiana Infantry Regiments and the 1st Louisiana Battalion, photographed where they fell along the Hagerstown Pike at the Battle of Sharpsburg. Their single-breasted jackets are all plain. (National Archives)

53. Private J. P. Starcher served in the 3rd Virginia Infantry and 19th Virginia Cavalry. He could have been in either unit when this photograph was taken. The 3rd came from Portsmouth in July 1861 and served in all the campaigns of the Army of Northern Virginia. The 19th was raised in April 1863, serving in the Shenandoah Valley until disbanded in April 1865. (Tom Williams Collection/US Army Military History Institute)

54. This dummy wears an original Confederate infantryman's uniform and equipment and gives a good idea of what the typical infantry private looked like. The uniform is all grey wool, with seven brass buttons down the front, and the weapon is a Richmond-made copy of the M1855 rifled musket. The brass belt plate bearing the letters 'CS' was typical of western Confederates rather than of the Army of Northern Virginia. (Smithsonian Institution)

53 ▼   54 ▶

55. Private W. F. Henry, Company G, 6th Tennessee Infantry Regiment, wears the letters 'JG', for Jackson Grays (which became Coy G of the 6th), on the front of his grey forage cap. He is armed with a knife and a Colt revolver, neither of which would last long in actual service. The 6th was in the Army of Tennessee, Henry surrendering with his unit as a sergeant in North Carolina on 1 May 1865. (Herb Peck Jr collection)

56. This man, apparently a member of Ramseur's North Carolina Brigade, was photographed in May 1864 where he fell during the fighting near Spotsylvania, Virginia. The weapon is an Enfield rifled musket; the round tin canteen with rings pressed in its sides was US Army issue. His leather pouch for percussion caps, with a shield front, and his leather cartridge box next to it were worn on his waist belt. (Library of congress)

57. These three men appear to have been stragglers from the Army of Northern Virginia after Gettysburg. The three-day-long battle saw General Lee try to destroy the Army of the Potomac by hitting its right and left flanks and, finally, its centre on 3 July. That final, unsuccessful assault has gone into the history books as Pickett's Charge. (Library of Congress)

56 ▲   57 ▼

58. The piping on the coat worn by Private D. R. Cesar, Company E, 1st Local Troops, Georgia Infantry, is odd, to say the least. The waist-level pocket is used to hold the percussion caps, so no separate leather pouch is needed. The unit was raised in Augusta, helping in the unsuccessful defence of the State against Sherman's forces in 1864. (Lee Joyner collection)

59. The weapon lying over the body of this defender of Fort Mahone, who died in April 1865 as the Union troops overran the Southern defence of Petersburg, Virginia, appears to be a US Army M1861 Colt Contract Rifle Musket, one of thousands of captured US Army weapons used by the Confederate Army. The weapon behind him is a US Army smoothbore musket converted from flintlock to percussion cap – and still in service. (Library of Congress)

60. This typical set of Confederate cavalry uniform and equipment, complete with US Army-issue belt plate, is worn by Private J. P. Sellman, Company K, 1st Virginia Cavalry. The unit was formed in July 1861 and was highly feared in the early years of the war. Their charge into the 11th New York at the First Manassas was one of the turning points of that battle. (Charles T. Jacobs collection/US Army Military History Institute)

61. The sabre held by this Virginia cavalryman was made in the Virginia Manufactory in the early 1800s and pressed into service in 1861. His hand gun is a Remington revolver, made in the North, while his all-brass belt plate bears the seal of the State of Virginia. His collar probably has yellow trim with a single button on each side. (Herb Peck Jr collection)

62. Yellow tape is probably used to decorate the collar of the single-breasted jacket worn by Private Bently Weston, 7th South Carolina Cavalry Regiment. The 7th was organized in March 1864 from various understrength units and served in Northern Virginia until surrendered. By 1864, Confederate cavalry was generally outmatched by better-equipped, better-horsed Union cavalry. (Library of Congress)

▲58 ▼59

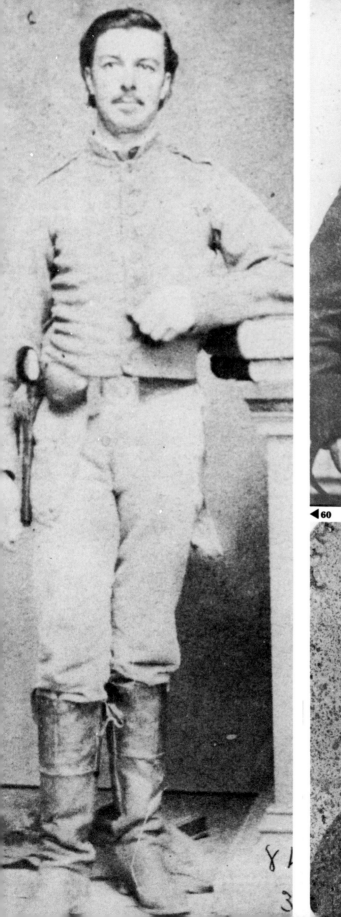

◀60   61▲   62▼

◀63 64 ▲ 65 ▼

63. Private J. O. Sheppard, Company F, 6th South Carolina Cavalry, wears a magnificently trimmed copy of the US cavalry jacket, with a US Army-issue belt and sword. He later became the regiment's sergeant major. The 6th, called the Dixie Rangers, was raised in January 1863, serving in South Carolina and then Northern Virginia, and finally surrendering with the Army of Tennessee. (Brig. Gen. James Daniels collection/US Army Military History Institute)

64. Private J. J. Dodd, Company C, 4th South Carolina Cavalry Regiment, holds a copy of the US Army-issue light cavalry sabre. Although issued, this weapon saw little actual use, most cavalry engagements being fought on foot with carbines. The 4th was formed from survivors of the 10th and 12th Cavalry Battalions in January 1863. It served in the deep South until transferred to the Army of Northern Virginia. It later went to the Army of Tennessee, with which it surrendered. (Library of Congress)

65. This well-armed soldier has a Colt revolver on his left and a Starr revolver on his right. Both are tucked into a belt made of painted canvas with a leather strap and brass or iron frame buckle on front. These belts came into being because of leather shortages in the South that forced their use as well as the use of shoes with canvas uppers and wood soles. (Herb Peck Jr collection)

66. These two members of the 6th Virginia Cavalry Regiment are armed with 0.36-calibre Colt 'Navy' revolvers. The man on the left has a percussion cap box on his waist belt, while the other wears a US Army cavalry cap badge. The shirts were often worn instead of jackets in 1861, but these home-made garments failed to last long into the war. The 6th served in the Army of Northern Virginia. (Library of Congress)

▲67

▲68

67. The jacket worn by this man, believed to be a member of the 1st Maryland Cavalry Regiment, is elaborately trimmed. Unfortunately, because of the chemical make-up of photographic film of the 1860s, the exact colours cannot be accurately determined. His checked trousers are certainly civilian, however, and his hat bears a plume, something popular with mounted troops. (Charles T. Jacobs collection/US Army Military History Institute)

68. The jacket and waistcoat worn by Private Francis Jones, 8th Virginia Cavalry Regiment, match in colour and, probably, material. The 8th was formed in early 1862 in western Virginia, serving there and in Tennessee before joining troops in the Shenandoah Valley. It was present at Appomattox but cut its way through Union lines and disbanded after the surrender there. (Library of Congress)

69. This detail of a photograph of a light artillery section abounds in uniform and equipment information. The officer, in the frock coat, carries a cavalry sabre. The man ramming, left, wears a round peaked cap, apparently an M1839 US Army forage cap. The day of muzzle-loading artillery commanding the field, as it had done in Napoleon's time, was past, since rifled muskets could bring down artillery crews before they could do much damage to infantry formations. (Library of Congress)

70. The man ramming on the right-hand gun in the two-gun section wears a red stripe down his leg, while the man standing next to him wears red pointed cuffs and, probably, a standing collar; the others in the section have plain, all-grey jackets. The sergeant, standing next to the young guidon bearer, has an issue light artillery sabre. (Library of Congress)

▲71 ▼72 ▲73

76▲

74▲ 75▼

71. It is not known what branch of service these men were in, although the dark trim on their coat collars and epaulettes and the dark forage caps with a lighter trefoil design on top suggest the artillery. Despite the uniformity of their coats, all three wear different coloured trousers. The white shirts and ties suggest that the photograph was taken in 1861. (John R. Wernick collection)

72. This motley collection is made up of prisoners from the Army of Tennessee awaiting shipment to a Northern prisoner-of-war camp. Confederate prisoners were not left unhoused and starved, as were Union prisoners, but they still died by the thousands in the cold climates of the camps. In all, 462,634 Confederates became prisoners-of-war, of whom 25,976 died in captivity. (Library of Congress)

73. Virginian Edward Thomas Hoge wears a grey jacket that appears to be made of cotton/wool mixed cloth with a collar of a facing colour, perhaps red for artillery. His buttons appear to be brass but are smaller than usual. A slash pocket over each breast is fastened with a matching brass button. (Hatsy Droke collection/US Army Military History Institute)

74. This soldier, photographed in Nashville, Tennessee, wears the plain jacket typically issued throughout the war. Officially grey, the shades of grey ranged from off-white to almost black. Also worn, at least until 1863, were brown uniforms, ranging from dust coloured to coffee coloured according to locally available dyes. (Author's collection)

75. This man's waistcoat is not only of a lighter colour than his jacket, but also uses small, brass ball buttons instead of the more typical buttons marked with branch-of-service letters or state coats-of-arms. Waistcoats were made at home rather than issued, and hence varied widely. Most, however, came with a small standing collar and three or four patch pockets. (Author's collection)

76. The trim on this Virginia soldier's jacket edges the top and front of his standing collar and then passes down the jacket front. This was a common feature of trimmed jackets or coats. By 1863 most jackets were made without branch-of-service colour trim, despite the fact that such was regulation. (Author's collection)

◀77　　　　　78▲　79▶

77. Commodore French Forrest wears the uniform of a flag officer in the Confederate Navy, with his cap peak bound in brass and the gold-embroidered fouled anchor within a wreath badge. His sword is a British-made regulation Confederate Navy model, as is his sword belt plate. Forrest was the head of the Navy's Bureau of Orders and Detail. (US Army Military History Institute)

78. Admiral Franklin Buchanan commanded the Confederate Navy's CSS *Virginia* in its history-making engagement with the USS *Monitor* and then commanded a small squadron in an unsuccessful attempt to defend Mobile Bay against an overwhelming US Navy squadron that included a number of *Monitor*-Class ships. His uniform is essentially the same as Forrest's, with an executive loop on the top gold-lace stripe on his cuffs. Buchanan's uniform now in the Maryland Historical Society collection, however, bears Maryland State buttons. (US Army Military History Institute)

79. Midshipman John Morris Morgan's rank is indicated by the three medium-sized buttons worn on each cuff combined with his lack of shoulder straps. A passed midshipman would wear a gold stripe on each shoulder. Morgan, however, wears the same British-made sword as Commodore French Forrest. Moreover, he buttons his coat at the collar in accordance with regulations. (US Army Military History Institute)

80◄

81▲

82▲   83▼

80. Although there are no known published Marine Corps dress regulations, it appears that most officers wore Army-style uniforms with dark blue as a branch-of-service colour. First Lieutenant D. G. Raney of the Corps also wears Russian shoulder knots, regulation in the US Marine Corps and common among Confederate Marine officers. HIs belt plate is a US Army officer's model. Raney was a Marine officer on the CSS *Tennessee* in the engagement at Mobile Bay.

81. First Lieutenant Frances H. Cameron spent most of his time in the Marine Corps on staff duty, although his first duty was with the Corps' Company A. His collar is folded down, so it cannot be told if he wears Army-style insignia on it, but the gold Austrian knot is regulation for his rank. His coat appears to be an unusually dark grey. (National Archives)

82. There are no known photographs of enlisted Marines; they appear to have worn grey frock coats with black trim on the collar and cuffs and a single row of seven buttons, along with plain dark blue caps. This man's uniform may be that of the Corps, with dark-colour piping around the collar and down the coat front as well as on the cuff edges. (US Army Military History Institute)

83. Marines in the Richmond area, part of the force defending against the 1864 assault towards the city from the Bermuda Hundred, were described as wearing jackets like those worn in the Army. This corporal's dark cap and chevrons (worn pointing up rather than down) suggests the possibility that he is an enlisted Marine. Revolvers were often issued for shipboard use, being easier to wield in confined areas than muskets. (George M. Cress collection)

QUOTES FROM THE GENERALS

I propose to fight it out on this line, if it takes all summer.

General of the Army Ulysses S. Grant, 11 May 1864, dispatch to Washington during the Battle of Spotsylvania Courthouse

•

However long you live and whatever you accomplish, you will find that the time you spent in the Confederate army was the most profitable spent portion of your life. Never again speak of having lost time in the army!

General Robert E .Lee, quoted in Freeman, R. E. Lee, Vol. IV, 1935

•

I do not propose to lay down a plan of campaign: but simply to lay down the work it is desirable to have done and leave you free to execute it in your own way.

General of the Army Ulysses S. Grant, 1864, mission orders to General Sherman for the destruction of Johnston's Army

•

It is well that war is so terrible – we would grow too fond of it.

General Robert E. Lee to Longstreet, Battle of Fredricksburg, 13 December 1862.

•

Wherever the enemy goes, let our troops go also.

General of the Army Ulysses S. Grant, 1 August 1864, dispatch to General Halleck about Sheridan's operations in the Shenandoah Valley

•

The art of war is simple enough. Find out where your enemy is. Get at him as soon as you can. Strike at him as hard as you can and as often as you can, and keep moving on.

General of the Army Ulysses S. Grant, (1822-1885)

•

I was too weak to defend, so I attacked.

General Robert E. Lee (1807-70) (attributed)

•

The true way to be popular with the troops is not to be free and familiar with them, but to make them believe you know more than they do.

General of the Army William T. Sherman 11 November 1864, letter to Rev. Henry Lay

•

If the entire Union Army comes across here, I will kill them all.

Lieutenant General James Longstreet, 13 December 1862, at Marye's Heights during the Battle of Fredericksburg

QUOTES FROM THE GENERALS

It is painful enough to discover with what unconcern they speak of war and threaten it. I have seen enough of it to make me look upon it as the sum of all evils.

Lieutenant General Thomas 'Stonewall' Jackson, April 1861, letter

•

What a cruel thing is war: to separate and destroy families and friends, and mar the purest joys and happiness God has granted us in this world; to fill our hearts with hatred instead of love for our neighbors, and to devastate the fair face of this beautiful world.

General Robert E. Lee, 25 December 1862, letter to his wife

•

I began to regard the death and mangling of a couple of thousand men as a small affair, a kind of morning dash – and it may well be that we become so hardened.

General of the Army William T. Sherman, July 1865, letter to his wife

•

The legitimate object of war is a more perfect peace.

General of the Army William T. Sherman, 20 July 1865

My troops may fail to take a position, but are never driven from one.

Lieutenant General Thomas 'Stonewall' Jackson, (1824-1863)

•

Then there is nothing left for me but to go and see General Grant, and I would rather die a thousand deaths.

General Robert E. Lee, 9 April 1865

•

No matter what may be the ability of the officer, if he loses the confidence of his troops, disaster must sooner or later ensue.

General Robert E. Lee, 8 August 1863, letter to Jefferson Davis

•

Bear in mind, the object is to drive the enemy south; and to do this you want to keep him always in sight. Be guided in your course by the course he takes.

General of the Army Ulysses S. Grant, 5 August 1864, orders to General Sheridan about the upcoming operations in the Shenandoah Valley, quoted in Sheridan, personal Memoirs of P. H. Sheridan, 1888

•

1. Major General Nathaniel Prentiss Banks wears the full dress uniform of his rank, complete with buttons in threes, gold epaulettes, and black velvet collar and cuffs. His sword is a non-regulation presentation model and his sword-belt is gold and black. Banks was a poor general, being driven out of the Shenandoah Valley by Stonewall Jackson in 1862 and thereafter commanding at the badly conducted campaigns of Port Hudson and Red River before being replaced.

CIVIL WAR UNIFORMS

A PHOTO GUIDE

Part Two: Union Forces

▲ 2

3. Major General J. Watts DePeyster served in the New York Militia. He holds a peakless pillbox cap which came into use during the war. His two silver stars are embroidered directly on to the uniform coat, without the black background or gold edging used in regulation shoulder-straps. This practice became popular for field use as officers so marked were less obvious to enemy sharpshooters.

3 ▼

2. Major General Philip Sheridan was one of the Union Army's three greatest generals, the other two being Grant and Sherman. He wears undress shoulder-straps with a silver star at each end. An 1853 West Point graduate, Sheridan had reached the rank of major general by March 1863 and ended the war in command of the Army of the Shenandoah.

INTRODUCTION

The American Civil War, which began when thirteen Southern states attempted to dissolve their bonds with the national government in late 1860-early 1861, was the most cataclysmic event in the history of the USA. More lives were changed, more soldiers and sailors put in the field, and more national institutions forever altered during the four years of that war than in any other period in American history.

This book cannot begin to cover the war in detail; it is intended, rather, to give the interested reader a look at the basics of those armed forces that fought to preserve the nation created by their grandfathers in 1776.

Photography had come into existence just over twenty years before the Civil War broke out. By 1861 photographers were to be found in every small town in America. Most of the two million of so soldiers and sailors had themselves photographed several times for family and friends. Many of these photographs have survived to provide historians with accurate data on uniforms and weapons.

While many men were photographed in dress uniform, a great number of photographs were taken in the field, where an enormous variety of dress – even civilian clothes – was to be seen.

US Army and Navy personnel of the period were not especially dressy; in fact, probably no war has seen less military-looking soldiers locked in combat. But the men were reasonably comfortable – or as comfortable as they could be in woollen uniforms in August in almost tropical weather – and the uniforms were convenient.

The basic US National military colour was blue. Soldiers generally wore dark-blue coats with, for dress, branch-of-service coloured piping, and sky-blue trousers (after December 1861), and dark-blue fatigue peaked caps or black, broad-brimmed dress hats. Officers wore much the same uniform, minus the piping. Sailors and officers in the Navy and Revenue Marine Cutter Service wore dark-blue dress that was very similar to that of the Royal Navy. Officers and men of the Marine Corps wore dark-blue fatigue caps or black dress shakos with dark-blue coats and sky-blue trousers with red trim.

Those were the regulation uniforms. There were, in addition, thousands of volunteers, wearing uniforms of virtually every imaginable colour. Grey was the most common colour among the volunteers, but these uniforms had largely disappeared from the front by 1862. Throughout the war, however, some regiments clung with pride to copies of zouave and chasseur uniforms often copied quite closely from those of the Imperial French Army.

Lasting four years and costing more casualties than all America's wars until Vietnam, the Civil War captured the public's interest to an extent unequalled by any other period in American history. Within the last two decades, tens of thousands of men and women have begun to attempt to recreate that period with authentically replicated uniforms, accoutrements, and weapons. Their efforts to bring the past to life are tremendous and it is to them that this book is dedicated.

Philip Katcher

▲4

▲5 ▼6

4. Brigadier General Joseph Hooker wears the uniform of his rank with his buttons in pairs, black velvet collars and cuffs, and a single silver star in the centre of his shoulder-straps. His sword is the regulation field officer's model, similar to that worn by line officers but lighter in weight. Hooker commanded the Army of the Potomac at Chancellorsville in May 1863.

5. Major General Franz Sigel, a veteran of the 1848 insurrections in Germany, was one of the leaders of the American German community, from which a large number of Union soldiers was drawn. His uniform is a common field one, even for generals, including the fatigue blouse and white leather gloves. Sigel was a poor general and was removed from command after being beaten at New Market, Virginia in 1864.

6. Colonel Silas P. Richmond commanded the 3rd Massachusetts Infantry on its formation in the autumn of 1862. He wears the regulation uniform for his rank save for the broad-brimmed 'slouch hat' with its infantry insignia and regimental number worn as a cap badge. The 3rd served along the North Carolina coastline, being mustered out in June 1862. Richmond then commanded the 58th Massachusetts Infantry.

7

8 ▶

Uniforms that varied from regulations were common, even among high-ranking officers. Colonel William R. Lee, commander of the 20th Massachusetts Infantry, wears a single-breasted coat rather than the regulation double-breasted version. His cap has a plain infantry horn without a regimental number. The 20th left Massachusetts on 4 September 1861 and served in II Corps. Colonel Lee resigned in late 1862.

8. Colonel Thomas Cass, commander of the 9th Massachusetts Infantry, wears a loose frock-coat buttoned down the front with four brass buttons; white gloves, and white canvas and brown leather 'sporting shoes'. The latter were a common variation from issued shoes. Colonel Cass was mortally wounded near Richmond on 27 June 1862.

▲9 ▼10

▲11

9. Major D. T. Eranto, 89th New York Infantry, wears his regulation coat in a fashionable mode for the day, with only the top buttoned. The 89th, nicknamed 'The Dickinson Guard', served from 1861 to 1865. The regiment saw service along the North Carolina coast.

10. This unidentified officer was photographed in the most famous studio of the day, Brady's Photographic Studios, in either Washington, DC, or New York. His rank is indicated by an oak leaf in either gold (for a major) or silver (for a lieutenant colonel) on each side of his standing collar – quite against regulations, but not uncommon.

◀12

13▲

11. Captain Nathaniel Lyon, 2nd US Infantry, wears the regulation dress uniform of his rank; he is holding his dress cap. His sword is the regulation line officer's sword. Lyon was gazetted major general on 17 May 1861 and organized and led the Union forces that saved Missouri for the Union. He was killed in action at Wilson's Creek, Missouri on 10 August 1861.

12. A regulation company-grade officer, photographed in Sing Sing, New York, as he would have appeared on parade and in the field. His line officer's sword is hooked up with the hilt towards the rear, which was the preferred way of carrying it. The star on his collar is, however, inexplicable.

13. First Lieutenant Levi Lincoln, Jr., 34th Massachusetts, has his small slouch hat on the table next to him. The 34th left Massachusetts on 15 August 1862 and served in the Shenandoah Valley until mustered out on 16 June 1865. Lieutenant Lincoln was photographed in Baltimore, probably at about the time he was demobilized.

▲14 ▼15 ▼16

17▲

18▲

14. These four company-grade officers of the 2nd Delaware Regiment give a good idea of the different types of hats and corps badges worn by officers of their grades. The two lieutenants second from left (Brady), and extreme right, wear their II Corps badges on the side of their slouch hats; First Lieutenant Thomas M. Wenie (far left), wears his on top of his kepi. Captain Charles H. Christmas has a plain, grey hat without cap badge.

15. This 6th New Jersey Infantry first lieutenant wears a commercially sold version of the III Corps badge on his left breast. It was made of silver, with the regimental number cut out of the diamond-shaped badge. Although this photograph was taken in late 1864 or early 1865, he still wears dark trousers (against regulations since 16 December 1861).

16. Assistant Surgeon William F. Reiber, 47th Pennsylvania Infantry, holds a non-regulation, eagle-headed sword that probably predates the Civil War by a number of years. It was not uncommon for officers to carry swords used by their fathers or grandfathers in earlier wars. Surgeon Reiber was mustered in on 30 October 1862 and resigned on 23 January 1865.

17. Captain DeWitt Clinton Lewis, 97th Pennsylvania Infantry, was photographed at about the time when he saved one of his men from drowning under fire at the battle of Secessionville, South Carolina, which act earned him the Medal of Honor. This award was given to four men of the 97th, the only regiment to be enlisted for three years in Pennsylvania's Chester County.

18. First Lieutenant James J. Skiles, 97th Pennsylvania Infantry, was promoted from the ranks on 27 May 1863, and was wounded at Petersburg on 16 June 1864. He holds a foot officer's sword with a brass scabbard; most of these swords came with leather scabbards. His hat is an unusual one. The 97th was in X Corps in Florida, the Carolinas and around Richmond.

▲19

▲20   ▼21

19. First Lieutenant D. Divine, 143rd New York Infantry, was photographed in April 1864 in dark-blue trousers that had been against regulations for his rank for almost three years. The 143rd was part of VII Corps doing picket duty at White House Landing, Virginia, until reassigned to XI Corps on 14 July 1863.

20. The cap badge on this first lieutenant's dress cap (beside him) indicates membership of the 56th Pennsylvania Infantry. The regiment was mustered in on 1 September 1861 and fought at South Mountain, Fredericksburg, Chancellorsville and Brandy Station before being the first infantry regiment on the scene at Gettysburg in I Corps. There it lost 130 officers and men of the 252 who went into that battle.

21. Officers, such as this captain of the Veteran Reserve Corps, complained that the sky-blue coats with black velvet collars and cuffs became too easily soiled. By the war's end, VRC officers were allowed the same dark-blue coats as other officers wore. The VRC was considered an élite corps and was made up of veterans incapable of active service because of disease or wounds.

22▲

23▲   24▼

22. This man wears a regulation company-grade officer's coat without rank badges. His sword is the style worn by medical and pay department officers. His cap badge, however, is that of an enlisted infantryman. He wears white canvas and brown leather sporting shoes. This type of non-regulation dress was not at all uncommon.

23. Captain Harry Sleeper, 10th Massachusetts Artillery, wears the regulation shell jacket with gold Russian shoulder-knots of a light artillery officer. The 10th left Massachusetts on 2 October 1862, serving in the Army of the Potomac at Kelly's Ford, in the Wilderness, and Hatcher's Run. The last artillery round to be fired by II Corps and, with one exception, by the Army of the Potomac, came from the 10th. It was mustered out on 9 June 1865.

24. Company-grade officers often wore custom-made copies of the issue fatigue blouse. Captain G. Eland, for example, wore such a blouse with a black-lined collar that could be folded down for comfort. For more formal occasions, the blouse could be worn with the collar up to make a short dress coat.

25. This New York first lieutenant wears a custom-made four-button blouse with a breast pocket for a handkerchief. The blouse worn like this was very similar to the civilian day coat worn by businessmen of the period. The top of a military-style waistcoat with its standing collar can be seen just below his stiff, white shirt collar.

26. According to the 1861 dress regulations: 'Oficers are permitted to wear a plain dark-blue body-coat, with the button designating their respective corps, regiments, or departments, without any other mark or ornament upon it. Such a coat, however, is not to be considered as a dress for any military purpose.' Such is what this first lieutenant wears.

27▲ 29▼

28▲

27. This medical cadet wears his rank insignia on his shoulders with a green stripe around his kepi which shows that he is in the Ambulance Corps of the Army of the Potomac or Army of the Cumberland. The short jacket was often worn in the field as a more comfortable alternative dress.

28. The three buttons and stripe around this first, or orderly sergeant's cuffs are not regulation (and cannot be explained), neither is the large stripe under his standing collar. However, the chevrons are perfectly regulation for that grade.

29. A number of non-regulation non-commissioned officer's chevrons appeared during the war, of which this is one example. This particular design was used by the commissary sergeant of the 20th Connecticut Infantry. The half-chevron on each cuff indicates three years' service. The frock coat is plain, without the regulation branch-of-service coloured piping.

30. A perfectly regulation 1861 infantry sergeant, photographed in Philadelphia, holding his forage cap. His non-commissioned officer's sword hangs from a frog on his waistbelt – many other non-commissioned officers preferred the shoulder-belt for the sword. Note the wide, sky-blue stripe down each trouser leg.

31. Massachusetts' soldiers, such as this sergeant, often

appeared in dress frock-coats that differed from regulation in that the branch-of-service coloured piping on each cuff ran parallel to the sleeve bottom, not coming to a point on the front of the sleeve as per regulations. This sergeant does not wear the regulation trouser stripe. The company letter 'I' can be made out on his forage cap top.

32 ▲ 33 ▼

34 ▲

32. Most chevrons were made by sewing stripes of cloth on a dark-blue background and then sewing the background to the sleeves. This Maryland sergeant wears chevrons made from one large piece of sky-blue cloth with dark-blue lines chain-stitched at parallel intervals to give the same effect. In some cases, stripes of branch-of-service colour were sewn directly on to the sleeves themselves.

33. This West Chester, Pennsylvania corporal wears service chevrons on each cuff which indicates war-time service. They are sky-blue edged with red. His cap apparently bears the letters 'PVV', probably standing for Pennsylvania Veteran Volunteer. The sky-blue military-style waistcoat he wears was not issued, but most men liked to wear them and had them sent from home.

34. In 1861 Connecticut issued its first regiments with locally made frock-coats without regulation branch-of-service colour piping. This New Haven corporal wears one of them. These early uniforms were made of cheap, rough cloth which wore out very quickly. The 1st Connecticut returned from the First Bull Run, after three months' service, in trousers made from old blankets, captured Confederate zouave dress, and various rags.

▲35 ▼36

▲37

35. Musicians wore their dress uniform coats or jackets with an additional adornment. It included branch-of-service coloured piping from each coat button, edged by the same piping, 'the whole presenting something of what is called the herring-bone form . . .' This infantry musician also wears the dress brass shoulder-scales demanded by regulations.

36. According to regulations, the dress hat, as worn here by the private on the left, was to be 'looped up on the left side' in the infantry and artillery, and on the other side for all other branches of service. Feathers were to be worn on the opposite side. In practice, these hat brims were worn hooked up on either side, it not being clear whether the left side as worn or as seen was meant.

37. Soldiers usually had a choice of taking their dress-frock coat or fatigue blouse into the field with them. In the Army of the Potomac, some 46 per cent wore their dress coats instead of fatigue blouses.

Private George M. Stevens, 9th New Hampshire Infantry, as was true of the majority of New Hampshire men, preferred the dress coat. Stevens is armed with an M1841 rifle, the 'Mississippi Rifle'.

38. Private Harry Gordrick shows how the foot soldier's dress coat could be worn as a civilian-style outfit, with its standing collar folded down. He wears only seven buttons on his dark-blue waistcoat with its standing collar; most of these waiscoats had nine buttons.

39. The type of red-trimmed zouave jacket worn by this sergeant of the 95th Pennsylvania Infantry, nicknamed 'Gosline's Zouaves', was also worn by soldiers in the 69th Pennsylvania Infantry (with green trim) and 72nd Pennsylvania Infantry (with red trim). This sergeant wears the VI Corps badge on his waistcoat. The 95th mustered in during October 1861 and served in the Army of the Potomac until its demobilization on 17 June 1865.

▲40 ▼41

▲42

40. The 95th Pennsylvania Infantry's zouave jacket was not worn over an issue waistcoat, although some of the men acquired waistcoats to wear with their jackets. Often, therefore, the men wore fancy shirts, such as this man's which buttons all the way down the front with brass ball buttons like that worn on the jacket.

41. Some eight per cent of the Army of the Potomac's infantrymen wore waist-length jackets in the field. Many were cut such as the one worn by the regimental quartermaster sergeant. His jacket has state-issue buttons but is made without trim. He carried the non-commissioned officer's sword and has veteran stripes on each cuff.

42. For dress, mounted enlisted men, such as this light artilleryman, wore uniform jackets trimmed with branch-of-service coloured piping around the collar, cuffs, front and bottom, and back seams. Volunteers preferred a lower collar and often had their jacket collars cut down with only a single buttonhole of lace on each side.

43▲ 44▼

45▲

43. The mounted man's regulation dress jacket had two buttons and false buttonholes made from branch-of-service coloured piping, as worn by this man. In the field many mounted men, too, preferred the broad-brimmed slouch hats to issue peaked caps. This man also appears to wear the issue grey flannel shirt, which was cut pullover fashion.

44. Corporal Windsor B. Smith, 1st Maine Cavalry, wears the mounted man's dress jacket with only the top two buttons fastened, a common practice. Smith joined the regiment's Company 'K' in September 1862; was promoted to corporal on 1 July 1863; was captured around Petersburg on 29 September 1864; was exchanged April 1865; and was discharged on 24 July 1865.

45. This oddly trimmed jacket and large cap badge was worn by members of the 8th Pennsylvania Cavalry. The unit was raised as mounted rifles in mid-1861 and served with the Army of the Potomac. In the advance at Chancellorsville, performing a hopeless charge against Jackson's flanking force, the unit lost 150 men. The 8th served in 135 battles, a record equalled by only one other command in the Union Army. It was mustered out on 11 August 1865.

CHRONOLOGY

Note that some battles were given different names by the opposing sides. What the Confederates called Sharpsburg, the Union forces called Antietam. Union names have been used in this list.

1860
6 November: Abraham Lincoln elected US President.

1861
13 March: Army dress regulations issued.

12–13 April: Siege of Fort Sumter, South Carolina (CS victory).

15 April: President calls for 75,000 volunteers to put down the rebellion.

19 April: Blockade of Southern ports declared.

9 May: US Naval Academy moved to Newport, Rhode Island.

9 June: US Sanitary Commission formed for soldier relief.

21 July: First Battle of Bull Run (CS victory).

9 August: Army orders 10,000 *chasseurs à pied* (light infantry) uniforms from M. Alexis Godillot of Paris.

10 August: All Army mounted units made cavalry regiments, numbered 1 to 6.

12–13 September: Battle of Cheat Mountain, Virginia (US victory).

7 November: Capture of Port Royal, South Carolina.

14 November: US Christian Commission for soldier relief formed in New York City.

21 November: Army chaplains authorized plain black frock-coats, trousers and hat.

25 November: Army officers authorized use of enlisted mounted men's overcoats in the field.

16 December: Sky-blue trousers made Army-wide regulation to replace dark-blue trousers.

1862
6–16 February: Forts Henry and Donelson captured (US victory).

6–8 March: Battle of Pea Ridge, Arkansas (US victory).

8 March: Army of Potomac divided into five Corps.

9 March: USS *Monitor* stands off CSS *Virginia* (US victory).

14 March: Capture of New Bern, North Carolina.

28 March: Battle of Glorieta Pass, New Mexico (US victory).

5 April to 2 July: Peninsula campaign against Richmond (CS victory).

6–7 April: Battle of Shiloh, Tennessee (US victory).

7 April: Island No. 10 captured.

16 April: Slaves in District of Columbia freed.

29 April: New Orleans occupied.

10 May: Norfolk, Virginia occupied.

5 June: Army Hospital Corps authorized.

18 June: Double-breasted jacket with two rows of six medium-sized buttons authorized for Navy leading petty officers.

1 July: First national income tax authorized.

2 July: Government calls for 300,000 volunteers for three years' service.

16 July: Navy ranks of rear admiral, commodore, lieutenant commander, and ensign created; new insignia authorized.

4 August: Draft of 300,000 men ordered by Secretary of War.

26–27 August: Second Battle of Bull Run (CS victory).

18 August: Indian uprising in Minnesota.

17 September: Battle of Antietam (draw, but an effective US victory).

23 September: Emancipation Proclamation frees slaves in revolting states, effective 1 January 1863.

8 October: Battle of Perryville (US victory).

November: First black regiments formed.

13 December: Battle of Fredericksburg (CS victory).

31 December to 2 January: Battle of Murfreesboro (US victory).

1863
26 January: Recruiting of blacks in Massachusetts authorized.

28 February: USS *Montauk* destroys CSS *Nashville*.

3 March: Writ of Habeas Corpus suspended, conscription measure passed; Army Signal Corps created.

21 March: Badges for different Army of Potomac Corps ordered.

28 April: Invalid Corps, later Veteran Reserve Corps, created.

1–3 May: Battle of Chancellorsville (CS victory).

14 May: Jackson, Mississippi captured.

16 May: Battle of Champion's Hill (US victory).

23 May: Navy authorizes new officer insignia using narrow gold stripes; line officers to wear a star over the stripes.

25 June: Veteran Volunteers, men with three years' service, authorized service half-chevrons.

1–3 July: Battle of Gettysburg (US victory).

4 July: Vicksburg captured, River Mississippi in US hands.

13–14 July: New York draft riots.

1 September: Little Rock, Arkansas captured.

4 September: Knoxville, Tennessee captured.

19–20 September: Battle of Chickamauga (CS victory).

27 October to 7 November: First Sanitary Fair held to benefit Sanitary Commission in Chicago.

6 November: Brownsville, Texas captured.

19 November: Lincoln delivers Gettysburg Address.

25 November: Lookout Mountain overrun, Chattanooga freed.

8 December: Pardons promised for surrendering CS officials.

1864
6 January: Canyon de Chelly Campaign against Navajos in New Mexico, ends in Indian defeat.

11 March: Army Ambulance Corps created by Congress.

3 May: Wilderness campaign begins; fighting in Virginia will not end until Lee surrenders.

13 May: Battle of Resaca, first major battle in Atlanta campaign.

8 June: Lincoln nominated for second term.

19 June: USS *Kearsage* sinks CSS *Albama* off French coast.

11 July: Southern raid on Washington defeated.

22 July: Battle of Atlanta (US victory).

5 August: CSS *Tennessee* captured.

20 August: Revenue Cutter Service officers receive ½inch gold stripes for rank insignia.

25 August: Army chaplains authorized black braid herringbone design on their frock-coats.

29 August: Democrats nominate George B. McClellan for president.

1 September: Confederates abandon Atlanta.

19 September: Battle of Winchester, Virginia (US victory).

7 October: USS *Wachusett* sinks CSS *Florida* off Brazil.

19 October: Battle of Cedar Creek, Virginia; Shenandoah Valley secured.

19 October: Confederates in Canada raid St. Albans, Vermont, in the most northerly action of the war.

8 November: Abraham Lincoln re-elected to presidency.

16 November: Sherman begins march from Atlanta to Savannah on the Georgia coast.
28 November: Veteran Volunteer Corps, made up of discharged veterans, authorized; was never fully organized.
29 November: Colorado cavalry massacres peaceful Cheyennes at Sand Creek, Colorado.
15–16 December: Battle of Nashville; Southern Army of Tennessee destroyed.
20 December: Confederates abandon Savannah, Georgia.
21 December: Navy rank of vice admiral created; David Farragut named first to hold the rank.

1865
14 January: Navy authorized sack coats for officers.
15 January: Fort Fisher, last Southern port, falls.
3 February: Unsuccessful peace conference at Hampton Roads, Virginia.
17 February: Columbia, capital of South Carolina, captured.
18 February: Charleston, South Carolina, where war began, captured.
4 March: Lincoln inaugurated to second term.
21 March: Battle of Bentonville, North Carolina, last major battle of the war (US victory).
1 April: Battle of Five Forks, Virginia (US victory).
3 April: Richmond, Virginia, Southern capital, captured.
4 April: Lincoln visits Richmond.
9 April: Army of Northern Virginia surrenders to the Army of the Potomac.
12 April: Mobile, Alabama, last major Southern city in Confederate hands, captured.
14 April: Lincoln shot by actor John Wilkes Booth.
26 April: Joseph Johnston's army surrenders.
26 May: Trans-Mississippi Command surrenders.
6 November: CSS *Shenandoah* surrenders to British authorities.

CORPS OF THE US ARMY

Each corps contained at least three divisions; each division, three brigades; each brigade, usually five regiments; each regiment, ten companies; each company, 100 men.

I Corps: Formed in the Mountain Department 12 August 1862; discontinued 23 March 1864; reorganized 28 November 1864.
II Corps: Formed in the Shenandoah Department 12 August 1862; redesignated XI Corps 12 September 1862 while new II Corps formed in the Army of the Potomac on that date; discontinued 28 June 1865.
III Corps: Formed in the District of Washington 12 August 1862; redesignated XII Corps 12 September 1862 while new III Corps formed in Army of the Potomac on that date; discontinued 23 March 1864.
IV Corps: Formed in Army of the Potomac 12 September 1862; discontinued 1 August 1863; reformed from XX and XXI Corps 28 September 1863; discontinued 1 August 1865.
V Corps: Formed in Army of the Potomac 22 July 1862; discontinued 28 June 1865.
VI Corps: Formed in Army of the Potomac 22 July 1862, discontinued 28 June 1865.
VII Corps: Formed of troops under General Dix's command 22 July 1862; troops transferred to XVIII Corps 1 August 1863; reformed in Department of Arkansas 6 January 1864; discontinued 1 August 1865.
VIII Corps: Formed of troops under General Wool's command 22 July 1862; discontinued 1 August 1865.
IX Corps: Formed in Department of North Carolina 22 July 1862; discontinued 27 July 1865.
X Corps: Formed in Department of South 3 September 1862; discontinued 3 December 1864; reformed in North Carolina 27 March 1865; discontinued 1 August 1865.
XI Corps: Formed in Shenandoah Department 12 September 1862; consolidated with XII Corps to form XX Corps 4 April 1864.
XII Corps: Formed of troops under General McDowell 12 September 1862; consolidated with XI Corps to form XX Corps 4 April 1864.
XIII Corps: Formed in Department of Tennessee 24 October 1862; discontinued 11 June 1864; reformed 18 February 1865; discontinued 20 July 1865.
XIV Corps: Formed in Department of the Cumberland 24 October 1862; discontinued 1 August 1865.
XV Corps: Formed of troops under General Grant 18 December 1862; discontinued 1 August 1865.
XVI Corps: Formed of troops under General Grant 18 December 1862; discontinued 7 November 1864; reformed 18 February 1865; discontinued 20 July 1865.
XVII Corps: Formed of troops under General Grant 18 December 1862; discontinued 1 August 1865.
XVIII Corps: Formed in North Carolina 24 December 1862; designated to include troops from North Carolina and Virginia in the Army of the Potomac 17 July 1864; discontinued 3 December 1864.
XIX Corps: Formed in Department of the Gulf 5 January 1863; discontinued in West Mississippi 7 November 1864; discontinued 20 March 1865.
XX Corps: Formed in Army of the Cumberland 9 January 1863; consolidated with XXI Corps to form IV Corps 28 September 1863; reformed from XI and XII Corps 4 April 1864; discontinued 1 June 1865.
XXI Corps: Formed in Army of the Cumberland 9 January 1863; consolidated with XX Corps to form IV Corps 28 September 1863.
XXII Corps: Formed in Department of Washington 2 February 1863.
XXIII Corps: Formed in Kentucky 27 April 1863; discontinued 1 August 1865.
XXIV Corps: Formed from white troops of X and XVIII Corps 3 December 1864; discontinued 1 August 1865.
XXV Corps: Formed of coloured troops from Department of Virginia and North Carolina 3 December 1864; discontinued 8 January 1866.
Cavalry Corps, Army of the Potomac: Formed 15 April 1863.

SQUADRONS OF THE US NAVY

North Atlantic Squadron: Formed to blockade the Virginia and North Carolina coasts.
South Atlantic Squadron: Formed to blockade the Atlantic coast from North Carolina to Cape Florida.
East Gulf Squadron: Formed 21 February 1862 to blockade the southern and western Florida peninsula.

A: The Model 1858 canteen was an oblate spheroid tin canteen covered with grey, brown or blue wool, and suspended by a white cotton sling. A maker's name usually appeared on the pewter spout into which was placed a cork with an iron ring keeper. This canteen replaced earlier tin drum style, india rubber, leather, and wood canteens, such as the one to the left of the M1858 model, as the standard canteen some years before the war. Some wood canteens such as seen here saw limited, militia use by Union forces.

B: This private in the 9th New York Volunteer Infantry Regiment wears a typical Union Army copy of French zouave dress. The plain felt fez was red with a blue tassel; the jacket, waistcoat and trousers were all dark-blue trimmed in magenta; the sash was magenta; and the leggings were white. Red trousers were more typical, especially among zouave units that had imported French-made uniforms. The 9th was formed in April 1861, serving at Roanoke Island, North Carolina; Antietam; and Fredericksburg, before being mustered out in May 1863.

C: The Colt 0.36 calibre 'Navy' revolver was the handgun of choice of most Army and Navy officers as well as being a standard issue pistol in all services. A handsome weapon, it had walnut grips, a brass trigger guard, and blued steel barrel, frame, and cylinder.

D: The patented Blakeslee Quickloader cartridge box was designed for use with the Spencer carbine. It was slung over the right shoulder to the left front side, hooking on the waistbelt.

E: Almost 95,000 Spencer carbines were acquired by the Army for cavalry use. The weapon was very advanced for its time, using fixed, brass cartridge ammunition that loaded into tubes, inserted into the weapon's butt, to allow the firing of seven shots before being reloaded. A rifle version also saw limited use by Union infantry.

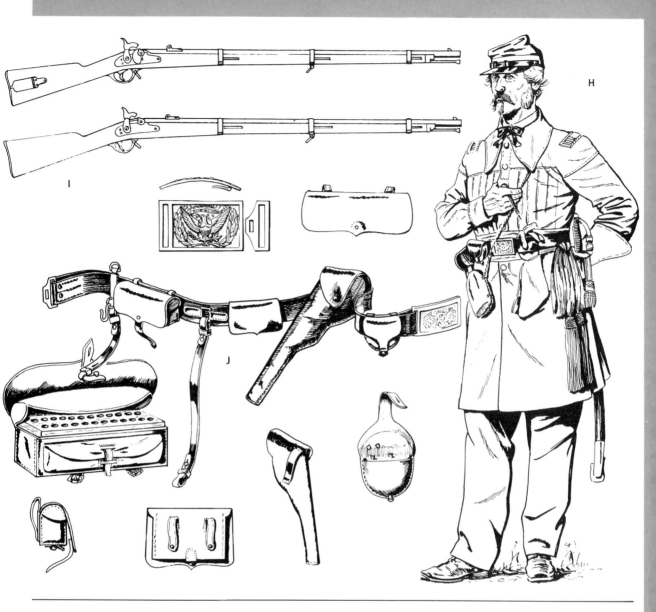

F: The issue haversack was designed to hold rations and, during campaigns, extra ammunition. It was waterproofed by being painted with a black, tar-like coating. A separate white food bag was held inside by means of three buttons, one on the front and two on the back. The food bags were often cut up for use as gun cleaning patches.

G: The Remington revolver came in Army (0.44) and Navy (0.36) calibres and was very popular because of the backstrap over the top of the cylinder which made it a stronger weapon than the Colt. A slight variation of the original Model 1861 version appeared in 1863, but both weapons looked very much alike.

H: Until June 1862 Rhode Island produced a state uniform for its two infantry regiments that included a dark-blue forage cap, a dark-blue hunting shirt and grey trousers. This captain wears the single-breasted version; a double-breasted version was worn by majors and above. His flask is a silver one, privately purchased.

I: The main infantry longarm was the Model 1855 rifled musket, seen left, and variations thereof. The M1855 featured an elaborate sight, a patchbox, and a patented automatic priming system which used percussion caps on a waterproofed roll of paper that was advanced with each cock. In 1861 a cheaper version of the M1855 appeared (seen on right). It eliminated the patch box and primer and included a three-leaf sight. Other versions appeared in 1863 and 1864 without the cleanout screw below the nipple and with an improved hammer.

J: The cavalryman's equipment included a sword belt with a brass belt-plate that bore the national eagle design within a silver wreath. The equipment on the waistbelt (not shown to proportion), included a leather pouch for percussion caps with a lamb's fleece that retained the caps; a holster (a privately purchased officer's model seen here); a small pouch for pistol ammunition; and a large pouch for carbine ammunition.

West Gulf Squadron: Formed 21 February 1862 to blockade from Pensacola to the Mexican border.

Mississippi Squadron: Formed to open and maintain free traffic on the River Mississippi.

Pacific Squadron: Formed to maintain the freedom of the high seas for American shipping in the Pacific Ocean.

West India Squadron: Formed to convoy California steamers; discontinued 3 October 1864.

THE US ARMED FORCES IN STATISTICS

Combat Units of the US Army

Cavalry Regiments	258
Independent Cavalry Companies	170
Artillery Regiments	57
Independent Artillery Companies	22
Independent Artillery Batteries	232
Infantry Regiments	1,666
Independent Infantry Companies	306

Strength of the US Army

1 January 1861	16,367
1 July 1861	186,751
1 January 1862	575,917
31 March 1862	637,126
1 January 1863	918,191
1 January 1864	860,737
1 January 1865	959,460
1 May 1865	1,000,516

Losses in the US Army

Killed	61,362
Died of wounds	34,773
Died of disease	183,287
Accidentally killed	306
Executed by sentence	267
Missing in action	6,749
Honourably discharged	174,577
Discharged for disability	224,306
Dishonourably discharged	2,693
Dismissed	2,423
Cashiered	274
Resigned	22,281
Deserted	199,045
Total casualties	912,343

Top Ten Fighting Regiments
(as indicated by total losses)

Regiment	Corps	Percentage Losses
2nd Wisconsin Infantry	I	19.7
1st Maine Heavy Artillery	II	19.2
57th Massachusetts Infantry	IX	19.1
140th Pennsylvania Infantry	II	17.4
26th Wisconsin Infantry	XI	17.2
7th Wisconsin Infantry	I	17.2
69th New York Infantry	II	17.1
40th Pennsylvania Infantry	V	16.6
142nd Pennsylvania Infantry	I	16.5
141st Pennsylvania Infantry	III	16.1

SHIPS OF THE US NAVY

Date	Ships	No. Guns	Tonnage
March 1861	69	1,346	unknown
December 1861	264	2,557	218,016
December 1862	427	3,268	340,036
December 1863	588	4,443	467,967
December 1864	671	4,610	510,396

WEAPONS OF THE US ARMED FORCES

FIELD ARTILLERY

M1857 Gun Howitzer (Napoleon): Adopted 1857. Smoothbore. Tube, bronze, 1,227 pounds, 66 inches long. Shot, 12.3 pounds. Charge, 2.5 pounds. Muzzle velocity, 1,440fps. Range at 3° elevation, 1,619 yards. 1,127 produced. A preferred antipersonnel weapon.

10-pound Parrott: Adopted 1860. Rifled. Tube, iron, 74 inches long. Shot, 9.5 pounds. Charge, 1.0 pound. Muzzle velocity, 1,230fps. Range at 3° elevation, 1,850 yards. 587 produced. Accurate at long range, especially for counter-battery work.

3-inch Ordnance Rifle (Rodman): Adopted 1861. Rifled. Tube, iron, 69 inches long. Shot, 9.5 pounds. Charge, 1 pound. Muzzle velocity, 1,215fps. Range at 3° elevation, 1,830 yards. 925 produced. Used much as were the Parrott guns.

INFANTRY LONGARMS

M1841 Rifle (Mississippi): 0.54 calibre, rifled, 52.66 inches long, 33-inch barrel, browned barrel, brass furniture. 25,296 produced. A common early war weapon, taking a sabre bayonet.

M1842 Musket: 0.69 calibre, smoothbore, 57.75 inches long. 42-inch barrel, bright finished iron furniture, 279,501 produced. Although obsolete, often used by militia.

M1855 Rifled Musket: 0.58 calibre, rifled, 56 inches long, 40-inch barrel, polished iron furniture, 39,792 produced. An excellent weapon, although the patented Maynard primer and elaborate sight made it too expensive for mass production.

M1861 Rifled Musket: Dimensions as above, 670,617 acquired by the Army. Essentially a simplified M1855 with a three-blade sight and plain nipple. Further variations were made in 1863, first by flattening the nipple bolster and removing the barrel band springs, then by replacing the springs. Many of these weapons were made by private contractors who also sold them to state militias.

P1853 Rifled Muskets: 0.577 calibre, rifled, 55 inches long, 3-inch barrel, bright finish iron with brass nosecap and buttplate and trigger guard. 428,292 acquired by the Army. The regulation British Army longarm of the period, these were the second most popular US Army longarm of the period.

M1854 Lorenz Rifled Musket: 0.54 calibre, rifled, 52.75 inches long, bright finish iron. 226,294 acquired by the Army. Made in Austria and lacking the quality of British- or American-made arms, many soldiers still thought highly of their lightweight Lorenz rifled muskets.

M1861 Whitney Naval Rifle (Plymouth): 0.69 calibre, rifled, 50 inches long, bright barrel and blued steel furniture and lock. The standard Navy-issue rifle, it came with a short-bladed Dahlgren knife bayonet.

CARBINES

Burnside: 0.54 calibre, rifled, 40 inches long, breechloading. 55,567 acquired by the Army. Four models, differing only slightly in appearance, of this weapon designed by Major General Ambrose Burnside, were used during the war. It used a special brass cartridge.

M1859 Sharps: 0.52 calibre, rifled, 37.75 inches long, breechloading. 80,512 acquired by the Army. The Sharps, which fired a paper-wrapped combustible cartridge, was one of the most popular carbines of the war.

Smith: 0.50 calibre, rifled, 39.5 inches long, breechloading. 30,062 acquired by the Army. The Smith broke open in the middle like a shotgun, using a rubber cartridge to prevent flash at the breech.

Spencer: 0.52 calibre, rifled, 39 inches long, magazine-fed. 94, 196 acquired by the Army. The Spencer used a tube magazine that held seven brass cartridges; the most technically advanced longarm of the period (save possibly for the Henry which saw little action) as well as the most popular carbine.

Starr: 0.54 calibre, rifled, 37.5 inches long, breechloading. 25,603 acquired by the Army. The Starr was very much like the Sharps carbine, in action as well as appearance.

REVOLVERS

M1860 Colt Army: 0.44 calibre, 14 inches long, 129,730 acquired by Army. The standard cavalry pistol.

M1851 Colt Navy: 0.36 calibre, 13 inches long, 17,010 acquired by Army. Preferred by officers, and was the issue Navy weapon.

M1861 Remington: Came in both 0.44 calibre Army and 0.36 Navy versions, 13.75 inches long (Army version). 125,314 Army and 1,901 Navy versions acquired by Army. The backstrap across its cylinder made this a more rugged weapon than the Colt.

EDGED WEAPONS

M1840 Heavy Cavalry Sabre: 41.5 inches long, brass hilt with leather-wrapped wooden grips, blade 1.25 inches wide at hilt, iron scabbard, 189,114 acquired by the Army.

M8160 Light Cavalry Sabre: 41 inches long, same as above but lighter, blade 1 inch wide at hilt, 203,285 acquired by the Army.

M1840 Light Artillery Sabre: 37–38 inches long, single brass guard and leather-wrapped grips, blade 1.25 inches wide at hilt, iron scabbard, 20,757 acquired by Army.

M1833 Foot Artillery Sword: 25.25 inches long, all brass hilt, blade 1.75 inches wide at hilt, leather scabbard, 2,152 acquired by the Army. A copy of the Roman thrusting sword.

M1840 Non-Commissioned Officer's Sword: 38 inches long, all brass hilt, blade 0.875 inches wide at hilt, leather or iron scabbard, 86,655 acquired by the Army.

M1840 Musician's Sword: 34 inches long and lacking counter-guards but otherwise a close copy of the NCO's sword, 33,531 acquired by the Army.

Officers' Swords: Cavalry and light artillery officers wore basically the same sword as did their men, with additional engraving. Foot officers carried the M1850 sword with an ornate guard and fishskin-wrapped grips in leather or brass scabbards. Medical and Pay Department officers had a special all-brass (except the blade) straight sword for dress occasions. The M1850 General and Field Officer's sword was quite like the foot officer's sword, but lighter. However, the M1860 sword for these officers was a straight sword in a metal scabbard with a quite ornate guard.

UNIFORMS OF THE FEDERAL FORCES

Army and Marine Corps/Navy Commissioned Officers' Insignia
(Worn on shoulder-straps, edged in gold, the insignia on branch-of-service coloured cloth for the Army; on black shoulder-straps, edged in gold with silver branch-of-service devices in the centre for the Navy; and on Russian shoulder-knots for the Marine Corps and Army Light Artillery.)

Major General/Rear Admiral: two silver stars.
Brigadier General/Commodore: one silver star.
Colonel/Captain: a silver spread eagle, having in the right talon an olive branch and in the left a bundle of arrows, an escutcheon on the breast (Navy on an anchor).
Lieutenant Colonel/Commander: a silver leaf at each end of the strap.
Major/Lieutenant Commander: a gold leaf at each end of the strap.
Captain/Lieutenant: two gold bars at each end of the strap.
First Lieutenant/Master: a gold bar at each end of the strap.
Second Lieutenant/Ensign: A plain strap.
Medical cadet (Army only): a 3-inch-long gold stripe, on top of a wider green stripe.

Army and Marine Corps Enlisted Men's Sleeve Insignia
(Chevrons worn above the elbow in branch-of-service colours for Army, points down; in yellow edged with red, points up, for Marines.)

Sergeant Major: three chevrons and an arc in silk.
Quartermaster Sergeant: three chevrons and a tie in silk.
Company Quartermaster Sergeant (Army only, after 1862): three chevrons and a single tie.
Ordnance Sergeant (Army only): three chevrons and a star in crimson silk.
Hospital Steward (Army only): an emerald-green half-chevron edged with yellow silk; a yellow caduceus in the centre.
First Sergeant: three chevrons and a lozenge in worsted.
Sergeant: three chevrons in worsted.
Corporal: two chevrons in worsted.
Pioneer (Army only): two crossed hatchets in branch of service colour.
Signal Corpsman (Army only): crossed signal flags, red and white (after 22 August 1864).
Ambulance Corpsman (Army only): green half-chevron (after August 1862 in Army of the Potomac, January 1864 in Army of the Cumberland, red in XVIII Corps.
Hospital Corpsman (Army only): green half-chevron (After 5 June 1862).

Army Branch-of-Service Colours
Artillery: scarlet.
Cavalry: yellow.
Engineers: yellow.
Infantry: sky-blue.
Medical: crimson (officers' shoulder-straps, black; hospital stewards' hat cords, mixed buff and green).
Ordnance: crimson.
Staff (officers only): black.

Army Cap Badges
(Embroidered on a black velvet background for officers, stamped brass for enlisted men.)

General and Staff Officers: silver Old English letters 'US' within a gold wreath.
Corps of Engineers: turreted castle (silver within a gold wreath for officers, brass for men).
Topographical Engineers: gold shield within a gold wreath.
Ordnance Department: gold flaming bomb.
Cavalry: crossed sabres, number of the regiment at the cross of the sabres (also brass Company letter for men).
Artillery: crossed cannon, the number of the regiment above the intersection of the cannon (also Company letter for men).
Infantry: a bugle, the regimental number inside the horn loop (under a Company letter for enlisted men).
Hospital Steward: white Roman letters 'US' within a brass wreath.
Signal Corps: crossed red-and-white signal flags under a silver torch and letters 'US' within a gold wreath (officers only; after 22 August 1864).
Sharpshooters: crossed rifles under Old English letters 'US' and over letters 'SS'.
Veteran Volunteers: seven-pointed star (after 18 June 1865).

Sashes
Generals: buff silk.
Other Army and Marine officers: crimson silk.
Army Medical Department: emerald-green silk.
Army and Marine First Sergeants and above: red worsted.

Army Corps Badges
Army corps badges were made from cloth or painted metal and worn on the hat top or side or left breast. They were first adopted in the Army of the Potomac on 21 March 1863. They were red for the corps' first division, white for its second, and blue for its third.

I Corps: a circle.
II Corps: a cloverleaf.
III Corps: a diamond.
IV Corps: a triangle.
V Corps: a Maltese cross.
VI Corps: a Greek cross (green for the 1863 Light Division).
VII Corps: a five-pointed star within a crescent.
VIII Corps: a six-pointed star.
IX Corps: a crossed cannon and anchor on a shield (green for the fourth division).
X Corps: the outline of a four-sided fort.
XI Corps: a crescent.
XII Corps: a five-pointed star.
XIII Corps: no badge adopted.
XIV Corps: an acorn.
XV Corps: a cartridge box with the motto '40 rounds' on a diamond.
XVI Corps: a circle with four bullets, the points toward the centre cut out of it.
XVII Corps: an arrow.
XVIII Corps: a cross with foliate sides.
XIX Corps: a four-pointed star.
XX Corps: a five-pointed star (green for fourth division).
XXI Corps: no badge adopted.
XXII Corps: a quinquefoliate shape.
XXIII Corps: a shield.
XXIV Corps: a heart.
XXV Corps: a square.

Army Zouave and Chasseur Regiments
The following regiments wore a variation of French zouave or chasseur dress at some time during their services.

Zouave Regiments: 11th Indiana, 33rd New Jersey, 35th New Jersey, 3rd New York, 5th New York, 9th New York, 10th New York, 11th New York, 17th New York, 44th New York, 53rd New York, 62nd New York, 74th New York, 140th New York, 146th New York, 164th New York, 165th New York, 34th Ohio, 23rd Pennsylvania, 72nd Pennsylvania, 76th Pennsylvania, 91st Pennsylvania, 95th Pennsylvania, 114th Pennsylvania, 155th Pennsylvania.
Chasseur Regiments: 18th Massachusetts, 12th New York State Militia, 49th New York, 72nd New York, 83rd Pennsylvania.

Navy Equivalent Rank
There were two grades of Navy officer, executive (deck) and civil. Each grade of civil officer had a unique title; they wore basically the same dress as equivalent executive officers with a special branch device on their shoulder-straps and minus the executive star over their cuff lace.

Commodore: Chief of the Bureaux of Medicine and Surgery, Provisions and Clothing, Steam Engineering, Construction.
Caption: Fleet Surgeon, Paymaster, or Engineer; Surgeon, Paymaster or Chief Engineer more than 15 years' service; Naval Constructor more than 20 years' service.
Commander: Surgeon, Paymaster, or Chief Engineer more than 5 years' service; Naval Constructor, Chaplain, or Professor of Mathematics more than 12 years' service.
Lieutenant Commander: Surgeon, Paymaster, or Chief Engineer less than 5 years' service; Naval Constructor, Chaplain, or Professor of Mathematics less than 12 years' service.
Lieutenant: Passed Assistant Surgeon.
Master: Assistant Surgeon, Paymaster, or Naval Constructor; First Assistant Engineer, Secretary.
Engine: Second Assistant Engineer.
Midshipman; Third Assistant Engineer; Clerk.

Naval Officers' Cuff Lace Insignia
Bars of gold lace worn on each cuff to indicate rank. A star was worn by executive officers in 1862 and by all deck officers after May 1863.

	1852	June 1862	May 1863
Rear Admiral	None	3 broad, 3 narrow bars	8 bars
Commodore	None	3 broad, 2 narrow bars	7 bars
Captain	3 broad	3 broad bars	6 bars
Commander	2 broad	2 broad, 1 narrow bar	5 bars
Lieutenant Commander	none	2 broad bars	4 bars
Lieutenant	1 broad	1 broad, 1 narrow bar	3 bars
Master	3 buttons	1 broad bar	2 bars
Ensign	None	1 narrow bar	1 bar

Revenue Marine Cutter Service Commissioned Officers' Insignia
(On blue shoulder-straps edged with gold.)

Captain: two crossed fouled anchors.
First Lieutenant: one fouled anchor over a shield in the centre with two gold bars at each end.

Second Lieutenant: one fouled anchor over a shield in the centre with one gold bar at each end.
Third Lieutenant: one fouled anchor over a shield.
Chief Engineer: an anchor over a gold wheel.
First Assistant Engineer: a gold wheel.
Second Assistant Engineer: a plain strap.

Revenue Marine Cutter Service Officers' Cuff Lace Insignia
Regulations in force at the start of the War had been written in 1843 and called for black cuff lace. This was changed to gold in 1862 and new regulations in August 1863 called for a gold Treasury Department shield over the top lace bar for all deck officers.

	1843	1862	1863
Captain	1 broad bar	2 bars	4 bars
First Lieutenant	3 buttons	1 bar	3 bars
Second Lieutenant	3 buttons	1 bar	2 bars
Third Lieutenant	plain cuffs	1 bar	1 bar

47▲

46. This cavalryman wears a plain uniform jacket (uniform jackets came to a point in front; shell jackets were cut straight around). This was a common type of mounted man's jacket; his has a left breast pocket. He carries a revolver in a holster on his right hip, and his sabre hangs from his left. A black leather pouch worn on the left front hip contains his copper percussion caps.

47. Eli Nichols wears the regulation uniform of a private in Company 'K', 9th Veteran Reserve Corps Regiment. The jacket is cut like a slightly longer version of the mounted man's jacket, in sky-blue with dark-blue trim. The 9th was part of the force that defended Washington against Jubal Early's attack in 1864 until VI Corps could arrive to relieve them. Nichols served in the 114th New York Infantry before being transferred to the VRC.

48. Since they were in permanent posts, VRC members sometimes purchased uniforms that were better made than issue ones. This private of the 13th VRC, stationed in the Boston area, wears a custom-made jacket whose trim is lighter than usual, and a kepi with his regimental cap badge.

49. New York issued its troops with a special uniform, consisting of a dark-blue, waist-length jacket with sky-blue trim around its standing collar and epaulettes. The 16th New York Infantry also received broad-brimmed straw hats in 1862, which they wore during the Peninsular Campaign. Partly because these made excellent targets, the unit lost 228 men during that campaign.

50. The New York State jacket had a slash-type breast pocket. State infantry regiments numbered 1-105 received these jackets which were made with sky-blue trim. Red trim went on the jackets issued to the first four state artillery regiments. These jackets proved highly popular, and men from regiments not issued with them still managed to obtain and wear them.

50▲ 51▼

52▲

51. Pennsylvania issued plain, dark-blue jackets to many of its men. This man wears such a jacket, and he has decorated the chinstrap of his forage cap with the brass numbers and letters '50 PV', for 50th Pennsylvania Volunteers. The 50th served in IX Corps, which saw service along the Carolina coast as well as with the Army of the Potomac.

52. A group of new privates of the 126th Pennsylvania Infantry had themselves photographed in their new, state-issued plain blue uniforms when the unit was mustered in for nine months' service in 1862. This man is one of their number. The regiment saw action at Chancellorsville.

53. This rather sad-looking private from Augusta, Maine, wears the standard fatigue uniform of the Union army – a plain, dark-blue blouse fastened down the front with four buttons, sky-blue trousers, and a plain, dark-blue cap with a varnished black leather peak and chinstrap and brass side buttons.

54. The issue fatigue blouse came with one inside breast pocket over the left breast that could be reached without opening the coat. This, however, was not sufficient for everyone. This private, photographed near Harrisburg, Pennsylvania, added to his blouse an outside breast patch pocket, closed with a brass coat button, made of an entirely different material from the coat.

5. The 1861 dress regulations alled for dark-, rather than sky-lue trousers, as worn by this an. The polka-dotted bow-tie rther indicates that he has een in service only a short me. His sky-blue overcoat is the chair next to him, topped y his fatigue cap with a mpany letter 'A' and gimental number.

56. Enlisted men, like officers, often preferred custom-made versions of the fatigue blouse. This hospital steward wears such a blouse, with two side pockets and one breast pocket. He holds a narrow-brimmed slouch hat. His green half chevrons edged with yellow, bearing a caduceus in the centre, indicate his grade. He was photographed in Harrisburg, Pennsylvania.

▲58

57. This Lewisburg, Pennsylvania, sergeant wears another version of the custom-made fatigue blouse. He also has three pockets on the outside and sky-blue chevrons on each sleeve. He wears a dark-blue military-style waistcoat, as well.

58. Private Alister M. Grant, a 'gentleman' from Philadelphia by profession, shows the uniform he wore as a member of Landis' Pennsylvania Battery during the Gettysburg campaign – complete with mud on the trouser legs. The militia battery members wore light-grey slouch hats with red hat cords, and fatigue blouses with five buttons on the front.

59. This private from Bordentown, New Jersey, wears a long version of the custom blouse that was apparently uniform to his regiment. A III Corps member, his cap badge is hidden under the rubber rain cover over his forage cap. This cover fastened to the side buttons and fitted snugly over the rest of the cap, leaving only the peak revealed.

60. The 36th Illinois Infantry was distinguished by the unit's unique cap badge, the regimental numbers within a wreath, as worn on the front of this private's forage cap. The sky-blue waistcoats with eighteen or so small brass buttons were also unique to Illinois troops. The 36th, a IV Corps member, lost 739 officers and men during the war.

▲ 61

61. Bandsmen, such as these from Quakertown, Pennsylvania, often wore versions of the fatigue blouse with shoulder insignia like that worn by officers, although they were not commissioned. The original print of this picture shows the top of the horn player's forage cap to have been coloured red as were the shoulder-straps.

62. The officer's dark-blue overcoat had four black silk buttons and loops across the front and a cape that could be detached. Rank was indicated on the cuff; a plain cuff, such as that worn by this man from Jersey City, was for a second lieutenant.

▲ 62

63▲

64▲ 65▼

. Captain John H. Symonds, nd Massachusetts Infantry, s commissioned on 1 October 1 and discharged on 26 gust 1863. He wears a unique t-plate which bears the te's coat of arms and shows black quilted cotton lining the officer's overcoat. The nd served with the Army of Potomac's V Corps, in the ninsula, Fredericksburg, ancellorsville and Gettysburg.

. The single black braid on s officer's cuff indicates that is a first lieutenant, while the

silver letters 'US' within a gold wreath indicate that he is a staff officer. Each higher rank had an additional cuff braid, up to five for a colonel, so that a major's cuff would have three braids.

65. The enlisted foot soldier's sky-blue overcoat had a cape that ended at the elbow. The sleeves were made longer than necessary to serve as mittens, but could be folded up for convenience. Notice the side this infantryman's dress hat is looped up on.

▲67

66. The standing collar on the foot soldier's overcoat could be worn folded down; it was of the thickness of several pieces of cloth and tended to chafe the neck. This man is also wearing a watch-chain with his sky-blue, military-style waistcoat and a rather plain slouch hat.

67. Although the sky-blue trousers and dark-blue kepi on this man indicate that he is a soldier, his waistcoat and shirt are strictly civilian. Such white or colour checked shirts, usually red or blue, were quite common because most soldiers preferred to purchase shirts or have them sent from home rather than wear the grey flannel issue shirts of poorer quality.

68. Captain William B. Shubrick, Chairman of the Navy's Lighthouse Board during the Civil War, wears the dress coat for an officer of his rank, according to the 1852 regulations. He should also have worn dress trousers with a gold stripe down each leg. Only top-ranking Navy officers continued to wear epaulettes during the war.

69. Commander John L. Worden, who commanded the USS *Monitor* in its history-making fight with the CSS *Virginia*, wears the rank insignia style made regulation in July 1862 (until May 1863), with its combination of broad and narrow gold bars around each cuff. Worden also commanded the USS *Montauk* when she sank the CSS *Nashville* on 28 February 1863.

▲70

70. Since rank insignia regulations changed several times during the war there was often a mixture of different types to be seen at once. This commander wears a coat with the executive star over gold lace bars, one for each grade, authorized in May 1863. His hat, however, features the wide gold band and cap badge with an eagle within a wreath authorized in 1852.

71. Straw hats were authorized, and widely worn in hot climates by Navy officers. This officer, photographed after May 1863, would rate as a lieutenant commander, but the executive star is missing, indicating that he is a civil officer, either a surgeon, paymaster, chief engineer, naval constructor (less than five years' service), a chaplain (less than fourteen years'), or a professor of mathematics (less than twelve years').

▲71

72. The leaf design between two bars in the shoulder-straps, together with the two narrow cuff stripes without an executive star indicate that this officer, photographed in Gibraltar after May 1863, is an assistant paymaster. Because of that area's hot climate, he wears authorized white trousers and a detachable white cap cover.

73. The Navy had a number of warrant officer ranks whose equivalent in the Army would have been somewhere between commissioned and non-commissioned officers. One such rank was that of master's mate, who could command some types of small boat. This master's mate, photographed after May 1863, is distinguished by his lack of shoulder-straps, the cap badge consisting of a plain wreath, and a single star on his cuffs. Note the regulation Navy officer's sword.

▲74 ▼75   76▶

4. Midshipmen were distinguishable by the two fouled anchor badges worn on the collar. Like all officers, they were authorized to wear short blue jackets, but these were mostly worn at the Naval Academy and were abandoned in active service. This midshipman's cap has been covered with a rubber waterproof cover. His overcoat is on the chair next to him.

5. From 1852, clerks, such as this man, were to wear single-breasted coats with falling collars and a single row of six buttons down the front. Caps featured a plain wreath for a badge. A clerk was considered to be a warrant officer. The shape of the cap, with very little overhang, and its lack of a gold stripe, suggests a post-May 1863 date for this photograph.

76. The comfortable sack coat, copied from coats worn by civilian businessmen, became a standard, if unauthorized, sea dress for most Navy officers. It was finally authorized officially on 14 January 1865. It was usually worn with cuff insignia and shoulder-straps. The lack of such insignia, and the gold cap lace in this photograph suggests that the subject was a master's mate, some time from July 1862 to May 1863.

77. All chief petty officers wore the same ratings' uniform and badge of grade, an eagle on top of a fouled anchor under a five-pointed star. This petty officer is either a quartermaster, signal quartermaster, coxswain, captain of forecastle, or machinist. He wears a straw hat authorized in hot climates. Other petty officers wore the same badge on the other sleeve.

78. Dress of seamen, such as these two shipmates, was copied from that of the Royal Navy and consisted of dark-blue pullover shirts, plain trousers, and peakless caps. A black handkerchief was worn around the neck, often buttoned down under two small tabs on the front of the collar. A wide flap, often decorated with white stripes and stars, covered the back of the neck.

▲79   ▼80

▲81

82 ▲

83 ▲

9. The dress of US Marine Corps officers was similar to that worn by Army officers, save that all ranks wore double-breasted coats with gold Russian shoulder-knots with the rank insignia in silver on top of them, such as this worn by Lieutenant Mews, USS *St. Mary's*, a sailing sloop in the Pacific Fleet. Coats and French-type kepis were dark-blue; trousers were sky-blue with a red stripe down each leg.

0. The dress of Marine Corps enlisted men, such as this private, included a dark-blue, double-breasted coat with a standing collar with two yellow lace buttonholes, the whole edged with red piping; a brass fringed shoulder-scale on each shoulder (this man has removed his and the attachments for them are visible); and two yellow slash buttonholes on each cuff. For undress, an Army-type forage cap with a gold buglehorn around a silver Old English 'M' on a red crown was worn.

81. Lieutenant Jerry J. Benson served in the US Revenue Marine Cutter Service from 1843 until 1846. He was commissioned a second lieutenant in the Service on 12 November 1861 and was promoted to first lieutenant on 11 July 1864. His uniform is similar to that worn by Navy officers, except that the cap badge features a fouled anchor over the Treasury Department shield within a wreath. The Service was controlled by the Treasury Department in time of peace; by the Navy in wartime.

82. Volunteer militia units made up the bulk of America's military might in 1861. Virtually every town, no matter how small, had one of these outfits, which uniformed themselves according to their pleasures and pocketbooks. This lieutenant is from Worcester, Massachusetts. Militia units from that state often preferred grey uniforms, considering blue to be reserved for the regular army.

83. During the Civil War New Jersey raised its own Rifle Corps for local defence. For field purposes, Corpsmen wore plain grey jackets and trousers and had grey caps with black bands. Dress uniforms included blue jackets cut in the chasseur style, slightly longer than zouave jackets, with slits on each side.

▲84

84. Large cities had literally dozens of volunteer militia units, often quite old, each with a more eleborate dress than the next. This man's unit is unknown, although he was photographed in New York City. But his uniform, with its fringed worsted epaulettes, three rows of gilt buttons, cap with a pompom and the letters 'ER' within a wreath, white waist-belt, and lighter trousers with two stripes down each leg, is typical of many volunteer uniforms.

85. Uniforms worn by units raised immediately before the Civil War, when the forthcoming war was becoming obvious, were often much plainer than those worn by older units. This New Yorker of an unidentified unit, wears a very modern-style frock-coat decorated only by three buttonholes on each cuff and a small single button on the standing collar.

86. Mounted units were less common than foot units among the volunteer militia. Horses and their equipment simply cost too much for many volunteers. This Harrisburg, Pennsylvania private, however, belongs to a mounted militia unit whose short jackets had their collars decorated with a false buttonhole with a button on each end.

87. One of the most noted of all pre-war volunteer militia units was the First Troop, Philadelphia City Cavalry, founded in 1775. The unit saw short spells of active service on several occasions during the War. This Trooper wears the dark-blue dress coat with its red cuffs and standing collar, white lace, and silver-and-red sash. His Tarleton helmet, with its silver trim and black plume, is on the table next to him.